Spin Sucks

Communication and Reputation
Management in the Digital Age

GINI DIETRICH

800 East 96th Street
Indianapolis, Indiana 46240 USA

Spin Sucks

ISBN-13: 978-0-7897-4886-7

ISBN-10: 0-7897-4886-X

Library of Congress Control Number: 2013952804

Printed in the United States of America

First Printing: March 2014

Trademarks

All terms mentioned in this book that are known to be trademarks or service marks have been appropriately capitalized. Que Publishing cannot attest to the accuracy of this information. Use of a term in this book should not be regarded as affecting the validity of any trademark or service mark.

Warning and Disclaimer

Every effort has been made to make this book as complete and as accurate as possible, but no warranty or fitness is implied. The information provided is on an "as is" basis. The author and the publisher shall have neither liability nor responsibility to any person or entity with respect to any loss or damages arising from the information contained in this book.

Special Sales

For information about buying this title in bulk quantities, or for special sales opportunities (which may include electronic versions; custom cover designs; and content particular to your business, training goals, marketing focus, or branding interests), please contact our corporate sales department at corpsales@pearsoned.com or (800) 382-3419.

For government sales inquiries, please contact

governmentsales@pearsoned.com

For questions about sales outside the U.S., please contact

international@pearsoned.com

CONTENTS AT A GLANCE

TABLE OF CONTENTS

About the Author

Gini Dietrich is the founder and CEO of Arment Dietrich, a Chicago-based integrated marketing communications firm. She also is the founder of the professional development site for PR and marketing pros, Spin Sucks Pro. Gini is the author of the PR and marketing blog, Spin Sucks, which has been named the number one Cision Top 50 PR Blogs, the number three Listly Top 50 PR and Marketing Blogs, an annual Readers Choice Blog of the Year, a Top 42 Content Marketing Blog from Junta42, a top 10 social media blog from Social Media Examiner, and an AdAge Power 150 blog. She is also co-host of Inside PR, a weekly podcast about communications and social media, and where they all meet and intersect.

One of the top rated communication professionals on the social networks, Gini writes for *Crain's Chicago Business*, *OpenForum*, *AllBusiness Experts*, and for various PR and marketing blogs and publications.

She delivers numerous keynotes, panel discussions, coaching sessions, and workshops around the globe on the subject of communications in the digital age.

Gini is also the coauthor of *Marketing in the Round*, released by Que Publishing in May, 2012.

Dedication

This book is dedicated to Elizabeth Dietrich. When Marketing in the Round *was published, she said to me, "Honey, you are so sweet. Please don't let this success go to your head." I won't, Grandma. I won't.*

Acknowledgments

This book could not have been written without the Arment Dietrich team, who pushes me every day to be a better professional, to stay up on the trends, and to constantly create new ideas for our clients. Without the Spin Sucks crazies, as I lovingly call the blog's community. Without my parents who have blinders on when it comes to everything I do. Without Katherine Bull who encouraged me to write the book I've always wanted to write. Or without Kelly Dietrich who shamelessly tells people how proud he is of me. I'd also like to include a special thanks to Sean McGinnis, Jeannie Walters, Andy Crestodina, Mana Ionescu, and Shelley Pringle.

Thank you to each and every one of you!

We Want to Hear from You!

As the reader of this book, you are our most important critic and commentator. We value your opinion and want to know what we're doing right, what we could do better, what areas you'd like to see us publish in, and any other words of wisdom you're willing to pass our way.

As an associate publisher for Que Publishing, I welcome your comments. You can email or write me directly to let me know what you did or didn't like about this book—as well as what we can do to make our books better.

Please note that I cannot help you with technical problems related to the topic of this book. We do have a User Services group, however, where I will forward specific technical questions related to the book.

When you write, please be sure to include this book's title and author as well as your name, email address, and phone number. I will carefully review your comments and share them with the author and editors who worked on the book.

Email: feedback@quepublishing.com

Mail: Greg Wiegand
          Editor-in-Chief
          Que Publishing
          800 East 96th Street
          Indianapolis, IN 46240 USA

Reader Services

Visit our website and register this book at quepublishing.com/register for convenient access to any updates, downloads, or errata that might be available for this book.

Introduction

Consider this: The public relations industry might have begun in 1800 B.C. Back then, the Babylonians used stone tablets to educate farmers on how to sow and harvest crops. In Egypt, scribes documented the deeds of the pharaohs; in Rome, leaders such as Julius Caesar wrote biographies to persuade the public to support their political aspirations. There are numerous examples of persuasive speaking, the art of rhetoric, reputation building, and mediating between rulers and subjects.

Among the most famous was the use of public relations to promote Roman Catholicism during Europe's Counter-Reformation. Pope Gregory XV coined the term "propaganda" when he created *Congregatio de Propaganda Fide* (*Congregation for Propagating the Faith*), which trained missionaries to spread Catholic doctrine in the face of rising Protestantism. The term did not carry negative connotations until it became associated with government publicity around World War I.

Edward Bernays, the father of public relations and nephew of Sigmund Freud, worked on the women's cigarette smoking campaign in the 1920s. He helped the cigarette industry overcome a social taboo: women smoking in public. His client? Lucky Strike. His campaign? He persuaded fashion designers, charity events, interior designers, and others to make the color green trendy. Because a pack of Lucky Strike cigarettes was green, women would be more likely to carry them because the color was fashionable.

He is reported to have said, "The three main elements of public relations are practically as old as society: informing people, persuading people, or integrating people with people."[1]

Watch an episode of *Mad Men* and you'll see the PR theme carried throughout. Though the series focuses on an advertising agency, there is an episode where Peggy Olson suggests they create an event at the supermarket to get women to buy more ham for the upcoming holiday. They would hire an actress to grab the last ham from a shopper's hands, creating controversy and fabricated supply and demand.

Hollywood has not often been kind to the PR industry. *Wag the Dog* depicts a "spin doctor" (played by Robert De Niro) who distracts the public from a sex scandal by hiring a film producer to construct a fake war with Albania. In *Sex and the City*, the character of Samantha (played by Kim Cattrall) was a publicist who threw elaborate parties and spent her evenings club-hopping from fabulous event to fabulous event. And reality TV star Lizzie Grubman did the work of celebrity publicists in Manhattan while the world watched. She and her team of assistants planned nightclub openings, launched albums, and mingled with celebrities and the media.

Because of these depictions, when interviewing soon-to-be college graduates, their reasons for going into PR run the gamut from "I'm good with people" and "I love to plan a party" to "I'm a night person" and "My family doesn't mind if I go to events and clubs with clients."

There isn't a specific degree required to join the public relations industry. In fact, just about anyone can hang out a shingle and call themselves a PR professional. There isn't a global body monitoring the behavior of the industry, and advanced degrees and testing aren't required. That's why you hear so many stories in the news about the bad parts of the profession: astroturfing, lying, spinning the truth, making up fake personas to write reviews, doing whisper campaigns, sitting in on interviews so the clients can't answer questions for themselves.

Even business leaders hire PR professionals or firms, usually because they've heard from their peers that getting their names in the paper will solve all their problems. One year, two weeks before Christmas, we received a phone call from a man looking for a PR firm to help launch his new product. During the conversation, it came out that his expecta- tion was he would sell out by Christmas. How? By getting on the front page of the *New York Times* just a week later. Two weeks before launch date—let alone right before Christmas—is not enough time to get results, but he also wanted the front page of one of the most renowned and respected newspapers in the United States. Take a look at the front page. Have you ever seen a new product announced there? Typically it's reserved for world events, the country's latest crisis, or political exposes.

---

1. Barbara Diggs-Brown, *Cengage Advantage Books: Strategic Public Relations: An Audience-Focused Approach*, Cengage Learning, 2011.

Likewise, being in Chicago, it's impossible to count how many times prospects and clients would say, "If you could just get us on *Oprah*, all of our problems will be solved." Toward the end of her run, she only hosted authors and celebrities, but that never stopped business leaders in manufacturing, healthcare, software, and other business-to-business organizations from seeking the Oprah magic bullet.

The industry, as a whole, hasn't done much to change the perception that we're all spin doctors, liars, party planners, club hoppers, and magicians. The Public Relations Society of America (PRSA) is a membership organization for the industry. While it serves the needs of its members—professional development, conferences, networking, and content—it does not govern the industry fromas a whole from engaging in un-ethical practices.

The official definition of public relations, as redefined by PRSA in 2012, is: "Public relations is a strategic communication process that builds mutually beneficial relation-ships between organizations and their publics." But try to explain that to a business leader (or a young professional, or your friends, or an educator, or your grandma), and it goes above their heads. People understand what is tangible; media relations—when a story runs in print or airs on television or radio about you, your company, or your product or service—is easy to understand. You can see it, touch it, feel it. It's not something that feels like magic so it's often what is thought of when explaining public relations.

The truth of the matter is, while media relations is an important part of a communi-cations program, there are many other tactics used in a cohesive strategy: content, email marketing, social media, crisis and reputation management, events, social ad-vertising, investor relations, lobbying and regulatory work, and more.

That's why this book is called *Spin Sucks*. An offshoot of the number one (or number three, depending on which list you look at) public relations blog in the world, this book is written for business leaders who need to better understand how the industry is changing, what to expect from the PR professionals you hire, and what kind of return you'll have for time and money spent by hiring PR pros. If you are a communications professional, some of this will apply to you and some will be old hat, in which case your best bet is to check out the blog which is written twice daily specifically for you.

If you run an organization, are on an executive team, or have (or need to have) com-munications professionals or a firm reporting to you, this book will show you how to prepare your business for a marathon instead of a sprint, how to build a communica-tions program that can withstand the constant changes at Google, and how working ethically—while not providing instant ROI—will deliver more valuable long-lasting results, as well as a spotless reputation. You'll also learn how the lines between mar-keting, advertising, digital, and PR are blurring, and what to expect should negative criticism happen online.

Officially, the PR industry has only been around since 1929, and it has remained pretty much the same for more than 70 years. The tools today are different, but the premise remains the same. Lie or spin the truth, and you will be found out. People will take you to task. Your organization will suffer from decreased sales, lower stock prices, and a tarnished reputation. The digital Web has forever changed the way we communicate. It's changed the way we all do business. And it has forever changed the way we, the PR professionals, perform our jobs.

Tell Your Story Without Sex or Extortion

1

Sex Sells

The Kardashians. Miley Cyrus. *Honey Boo Boo. The Real Housewives. The Real World.* Rogue tweets. Lindsay Lohan. Michael Vick. Lance Armstrong. *American Idol.* Anonymous. Oscar Pistorius. Aaron Hernandez. *Sports Illustrated*'s swimsuit issue. The manhunt for the Boston Marathon bombers.

It's no surprise sex sells. And so do shootings and train wrecks and car accidents. It's the reason reality television and tabloids exist. We love the drama, the absurd, the ridiculous. It's the reason we're more interested in Beyoncé lip-syncing at President Obama's second inauguration than in the global state of affairs.

How often have you slowed down to check out the accident on the other side of the road or been stuck in traffic because of the rubber neck effect?

We're human beings. We love sex, tragedy, overnight success, the fall from grace, and the subsequent redemption. We moan and groan about the state of today's news, but ratings don't lie. Not only do we watch it, we share it far and wide.

When Laci Peterson went missing, not only were the media obsessed with the story, people around the world couldn't believe what had happened to this young woman and her unborn child. Many were preoccupied with the story and whether her husband had committed these murders. We wanted to believe she'd be found alive when that didn't happen. Can you imagine that tragic story turned good? Real life rarely happens that way, but Walt Disney made us believe, as children, there is a happy ending for everyone.

As organizations, we're faced with telling our stories in a way that is as compelling as sex, tragedy, the fall from grace (and the redemption), or the overnight success. It's nearly impossible to create those kinds of stories without a targeted communications strategy that is patient, flexible, and long lasting. Take the overnight success story as an example. It's impossible to tell it when you're in the middle of creating it, when you're working 18 hours a day and sleeping less than 5 hours a night to build something sustainable. You can't tell that story until it's perceived that you came out of nowhere and won the jackpot.

That's why *American Idol* and other reality talent shows do so well. They choose extremely talented people, give them rockstar coaches, and appeal to their competitive sides—and our own. From our perspective, it looks like they became stars overnight. What we don't see are the countless hours of auditioning and failing, performing night after night for free, or doing local theatre in the hopes of being discovered. That's not the interesting part of the story, though. We prefer to think it really is possible to achieve the American dream without hard work. That's why winning the lottery is so appealing and generates upwards of 60 billion dollars every year. We spend one dollar or five dollars with the idea, if we win, we can quit our jobs, move to an island, and drink fruity drinks for the rest of our lives.

But you don't have to have overnight success, a tragedy, or sell sex to be successful in today's media world. This book is called *Spin Sucks* for a reason. We are bombarded all day long, every day, with so many "spun stories," we end up with the perception you have to spin the truth, leave out uninteresting facts, or downright lie for that kind of attention. After all, the first few paragraphs of this book describe how well all of this works. But that kind of thinking, well, sucks.

If we look at *why* sex sells, though, we realize it's the stories that trigger human emotions or appeal to our reptilian brains that sell.

In 1885 W. Duke and Sons, a manufacturer of cigarettes, included trading cards in their packaging. Not just any trading cards, though. You didn't see images of Phog Allen or the Cleveland Blues baseball team. Rather, they used erotic images of the most popular female stars. Erotic back then, of course, was different from what it is today, but the point remains: There were scantily dressed movie stars on the cards. If there was a star you didn't particularly like, you could trade it for one you did.

Sales of the cigarettes increased significantly and W. Duke and Sons enjoyed one of the first word-of-mouth campaigns ever. The campaign worked so well, in fact, that the company grew to become the leading cigarette brand by 1890, and many companies still imitate the idea today.

But there's a fine line. If you bought W. Duke and Sons cigarettes because of the allure of the trading cards, but you didn't like the taste, you might feel cheated or manipulated. We are human, we respond to the things that appeal to our reptilian brains, but we're also very smart and become better educated—and more evolved—with every message thrown at us every day. If you sell with sex and your product or service doesn't work, not even scantily clad women will help your sales.

People are not rational creatures. We do not behave in predictable patterns. As much as we'd like to apply science to our communications, it's nearly impossible to do so. Relationships and brand perception matter. How a product or service makes a customer feel is important. What's most important, though, is how much trust you create through your communications: If you're using sex to sell something that hasn't created a level of trust, it won't work.

So, instead of sex, why not use your communications to build—and keep—trust?

Technology has allowed us to better understand our customers, their patterns, and even the human emotions that trigger the decision to buy—but there still is an art to communications. Business is personal. We buy from people we like and trust. Technology has allowed us to develop that trust through the content we create and in the way we communicate, but it's also easier for it to erode if we don't handle it with care.

Of course, this all worked differently before the digital era. It used to be that, if someone were upset about their experience with your company, they told their family, their next-door neighbor, maybe a handful of friends. They might even take the time to write a letter and mail it to the CEO, who might or might not ever see it. If the company had its act together, they'd send a letter back, offering to fix the problem in some small way, and that was the end of that.

Today, if someone has a bad experience with your company, they take to the Web. They tell their family, their next-door neighbor, and their 3,000 Twitter followers who all tweet and retweet the story until you're faced with a crisis—all because you were fed the idea that sex sells or that you have to spin the truth to gain a customer. While sex may sell the first time, it's a good product or service that sells the second time, and it's the trust you build with each customer each subsequent time that keeps them coming back.

Researchers at the University of Wisconsin at Eau Claire have found that Super Bowl ads with sexual imagery take a 10 percent hit in likability versus ads without racy images. Some of the biggest Super Bowl advertisers have spent millions on ads that exude sexual imagery, but most viewers prefer to see ads with kids or animals.

Advertising professor Jef I. Richards from the University of Texas says, "Sex sells, but only if you're selling sex."[1]

In the case of W. Duke and Sons, they used sex to sell their cigarettes, but if the product didn't work, all the scantily clad women in the world wouldn't have helped them obtain the lead position. If sex is used to gain attention, your product or service had better be actual sex or without any flaws. Otherwise, that instant spike in sales you saw will quickly evaporate.

---

1. www.versacreations.net/advertising/89/sex-in-advertising

How Communication Has Changed

In the good ol' days, you'd hire a PR firm or team to help you create your elevator pitch, your overriding messages, and supporting messages. Every person inside your organization was trained to say the exact same thing when talking to anyone about what you do. Your customers believed what you had to say about your product or service because you were the only one telling your story. If your PR team was worth its salt, soon the media—business, trade, consumer, radio, television—were telling the same story you told.

Now all it takes is for one person to have a bad experience doing business with you, and you're finished—both online and off. No amount of PR messaging can counteract that one person's negative experience.

Of course, there are many, many things you can do to repair your image with that one person who created a crisis for you. We'll cover that later in the book. But you no longer have control of your brand—or perceived control. You can no longer worry just about your marketing messages. You have to be in tune with what the customers say your brand is and how they define it to their friends, family, and social networks.

If you can do that *and* use sex to sell, more power to you. Most organizations, though, should be concerned instead with telling their brand story over a long period of time.

And it's not just your unhappy customers who can screw things up. What happens when you do just fine on your own? Have you ever heard the saying, "There's no such thing as bad publicity"? Whoever says that—and believes it—has never experienced truly bad publicity.

Your Customers Control Your Brand . . . and Your Messaging

In early 2011, Kenneth Cole tweeted, "Millions are in uproar in #Cairo. Rumor is they heard our new spring collection is now available online at http://bit.ly/KCairo—KC" (Figure 1.1). This was tweeted while protests were escalating in Egypt—and was not only disrespectful but completely ignorant.

The "KC" at the end of the tweet indicates that Kenneth Cole himself—not a marketing intern or inexperienced professional—sent the tweet, causing an uproar of its own in the Twittersphere. A couple of hours later, another tweet came from Kenneth Cole, with a pseudo-apology—you'll notice the words "I'm sorry" don't appear in the 140-character statement. The original tweet was deleted, but not before screen grabs were taken and journalists and bloggers wrote about it. More than half a million stories were generated, creating extremely bad publicity for the man and his company.

Just three weeks later, Kenneth Cole CEO, Jill Granoff, resigned unexpectedly and the company's stock dropped 9 percent. A little more than a year later, its stock was downgraded by TheStreet Ratings.

While no one directly blames the CEO resigning and the financial disaster on the rogue tweet, it's hard to point to anything else when you review the timeline. People

Figure 1.1   *Kenneth Cole tweets about Cairo and his new collection.*

buy from people they like and trust. Kenneth Cole has been in the business for more than 30 years and aggressively supports AIDS research and awareness, but one tweet created a reason for people to not shop there.

Warren Buffet said it best: "If you lose money for the firm, I will be forgiving. If you lose reputation, I will be ruthless." Thirty years of success upended by something that could have been easily avoided. If the tweet had been sent by a marketing intern, people would probably have been more forgiving. When it's the founder and chairman of the organization, people become vicious and even hostile. (An interesting side note is that Kenneth Cole tried this tack again in 2013 and, when called out, admitted it was to gain the publicity, good or bad.)

A year after the Kenneth Cole tweet, Susan G. Komen managed to go from a revered breast cancer research and awareness organization to someone completely reviled in a matter of 48 hours. On January 31, 2012, the Associated Press broke the story that the charity would no longer provide funding to Planned Parenthood. The decision was quickly determined to be a political one—the group's vice president, Karen Handel, ran for governor of Georgia in 2010 on a pro-life platform. Which, in and of itself, isn't a problem, but the controversy reared its ugly head with inconsistent communications, contradictions, and backtracking of the decision.

Denying it was a political move, the organization first cited a new policy requiring it not to fund organizations under government investigation. Then a public response—a YouTube video of founder and CEO Nancy Brinker—made things worse. Not only was it a well-rehearsed and calculated message, the background—a stuffy library—made it seem disingenuous.

A day later, Brinker told the *Washington Post* the reason for the funding cut was that Planned Parenthood did not provide mammograms to women, only referrals. That same day, a Komen board member flip-flopped the message again.

What started as an unpopular and poorly communicated decision became a crisis that resulted in the resignation of Karen Handel, the organization's president, Liz

Thompson, two board members, and Brinker herself. The nonprofit she had built in memory of her sister lost sense of its vision and handled the controversy poorly.

Six months later, they lost half their walkers, and sponsors continued to severe their relationships with the nonprofit. They ended up funding Planned Parenthood again, but the damage was already done.

This set the stage for an entire year of company leaders taking political stances. Oreo riled customers when it released a picture of a rainbow cookie to honor Gay Pride month. Chick-fil-A took heat for its president's stance opposing same-sex marriage. And the founder of Papa John's Pizza threatened jobs if President Obama wins re-election.

Don't be scared of communicating ever again. The good news is these types of crises are few and far between. Most of you will never have to deal with something like this. The better news is that you're now aware of what can happen and will be more cognizant of how controversy can be flamed by actions you can control.

So where do you start?

You have an incredible opportunity to build trust through communications, using technology to deliver it to prospective customers who would never before have the chance to buy from you. Does that make this whole notion a little more enticing?

Does telling your story belong to marketing? To public relations? To advertising? To content marketing? To social media? It really doesn't matter who owns it as long as the person or team in charge can tell a compelling story that is valuable, informative, and builds trust.

Tell Your Story Without Spin

Jay Baer of Convince and Convert has a great graphic, shown in Figure 1.2, that explains how a compelling story creates purchase.

The stories humanize the company, which creates kinship, which drives purchase. If done well, it also has another effect that is so desperately needed in today's world: It creates trust.

The 2013 Edelman Trust Barometer shows that the general feeling about organizations, having improved slightly from negative to neutral, is still one of distrust. Of course, trust is lower for financial institutions and media, but it's also weak for leaders and politicians globally.

The only way to build trust and slowly chip away at the bad feelings the general public has about organizations is to develop relationships and provide valuable educational information. That information should help your customers and prospects solve the problems they are having—such as weight loss, or work/life balance, or perhaps business growth or scaling more quickly. Whatever it happens to be, harvest stories that humanize the company in order to sell.

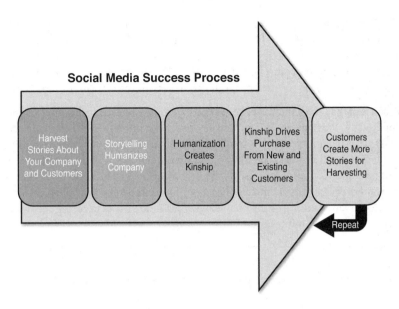

Figure 1.2   *The storytelling process from Jay Baer of Convince and Convert.*

There are many examples showing how companies grew because of the stories they tell: Zappos and delivering happiness, Virgin and their crazy founder, or Red Bull and Felix Baumgartner breaking the speed of sound in a free fall from space.

But what if you don't have big personalities or people free-falling out of spaceships as part of your story?

Foodily is an online recipe database, which you can use on your smartphone or tablet to keep all your family recipes in one place, plus get new ideas. Why would someone switch from an online recipe database they've already created?

Foodily knew they had to find a different way to entice someone to switch and to spend some significant time creating a new database. They quickly realized saying they are the largest online database wasn't the story—but giving you the opportunity to spend more time eating at home with family and friends was more enticing.

Founder Azita Ardarkani asked people to share, via the social networks, their favorite dinner table memories and what it means to them to eat at home. They began to see a natural conversation happen—one that didn't have to be managed or controlled by Foodily. What made it successful was the human emotion trigger. So much more than putting hot male chefs without shirts on their home page, she discovered a way to connect with people to build trust—without using sex to sell.

To create an emotional pull, she did three things with her story: expanded the idea of value, established a common language, and gave the brand a human voice. She humanized the brand to create kinship and eventually drive purchases—or, in this case, uses.

City National tells their story in a different way. They use employees and have created a contest to find the best of them. This came about in a very interesting way. If you look up the bank on Wikipedia, you'll quickly discover the story of Frank Sinatra's son who was kidnapped. The bank's first CEO, Al Hart, was a friend of Sinatra's and put up the $240,000 in ransom money to help with the return of Frank Sinatra, Jr.

Because of that, the bank has become synonymous with extraordinary customer service and loyalty. Particularly in Los Angeles, everyone knows this story; throughout the years it has become part of the bank's DNA. But chairman and chief executive, Russell Goldsmith—who comes from the entertainment industry—saw a need to grow beyond that one story if they want to scale the organization and be known for extraordinary customer service outside of LA. He set out to teach people how to share stories that were both entertaining and valuable, with the final goal of carrying the organization beyond that one famous kidnapping.

Every quarter they do a "Story Idol"—a competition among the offices, via the bank's intranet, where employees submit stories and everyone votes for the best. They receive 50 to 100 submissions every quarter, and then they have an annual competition where the quarterly winners are recognized in front of the top 300 people in the company. People tell stories about what they did to promote teamwork or how they helped a client by going the extra mile. Goldsmith describes it as telling stories around a campfire—only in this case, the fire is a conference room table.

Their website tells these stories, but it also goes a step further to help you tell your story. They build trust by creating humanization around the brand. They listen to their customers' experiences and encourage them to tell their stories. They inspire the best out of their employees because, in order to win, they need to tell an amazing story of how they helped a customer. They motivate their employees to provide extraordinary customer service—and that is a direct win to the customer!

Another company that does this really well is MailChimp, an email platform that helps you create professional templates, share your news on the social networks, integrate with your website, manage subscribers, and track results. It's one of the top email platforms due to its ease of use, ability to integrate with other programs, and price.

They take customer stories to a different level. In their own words, "We love what we do, and we have some amazing customers who love their jobs, too. That's why we've taken the time to get to know them and share their stories with you. These stories aren't about MailChimp—they're just short videos, articles, and photos that celebrate our wonderful customers."

If you visit their website, you'll find videos and photos lining the left-hand side of the page. On the right, there is a paragraph introducing each customer, describing who they are and what they do, and a link where you can learn more. Some of the customers naturally mention MailChimp in their stories, but it isn't a prerequisite. As you read—or watch—the stories, you'll naturally want to learn more about MailChimp, perhaps even try it out yourself. Not because they're selling to you but because the people who use MailChimp, and never even mention it, are so passionate about what they do for a living. It's a natural connection to think, "If they're so successful in their business *and* they use MailChimp, we should try it, too."

They've used their customers to tell stories to help build trust. Without sex. Without tragedy. Without violence. Their mantra is not "Any publicity is good publicity." They do it in a way that builds a romantic business dream and helps you believe even more in the American way. Suddenly you've signed up for MailChimp without even thinking why.

These are just a few really good examples of how organizations use stories to build awareness, generate leads, and eventually convert them into customers. Simply do a Google search for "customer stories" and you'll find pages and pages of results—organizations telling their stories. From big organizations such as Salesforce, Nordstrom, and Southwest Airlines to Sainsbury's, Trader Joe's, and Gaylord Opryland—all are telling stories, in real and compelling ways, about their history or leadership, or about their customers, or their customers are telling stories about them. The latter, of course, is the Holy Grail—but that won't happen if you sit passively waiting. You need to jump into the deep end and get started.

Use the Formula of Fiction Writing to Tell Company Stories

Fiction—both writing and reading it—is an underused tool for becoming better at storytelling. If you produce content, reading fiction is not a nice-to-have—it's a necessity. In fact, consuming content in general is a necessity. You should read Wally Lamb or Ernest Hemingway or Erin Morgenstern or Gillian Flynn, *and* you should read blog posts and articles and listen to podcasts, *and* you should read business books, *and* you should watch and read the news. If you do all of that *and* read *People*, you will become a natural storyteller.

Even if you don't produce content for your organization, the more reading you do, the easier it will be for you to see the organization's stories without thinking about it. Your team will love you when you come into the office with an idea for the next company story. Naturally curious people read a lot, which makes them excellent storytellers. People who don't read can't tell stories in compelling ways, nor can they expand their storytelling to imitate City National, or MailChimp, or any of the other organizations who do it well.

You can also cheat a little by seeing writer's movies. In the past couple of years, two really stand out: *Side Effects* and *Ruby Sparks*. But don't just watch the movies for entertainment. Watch them with that part of your brain that understands how the movies are written, how the script pulls you one way and then moves you to another, and how the characters are developed in a way that really compels you to care.

This is how you must tell your company's stories. *To tell great company stories, you must read, especially fiction.*

Mark Twain famously said, "Writing is like a disease—you have to get the words out of your head so you can live."

If you've ever been a writer—even if it was in high school or college—you know how what Twain said feels. Producing content is like that, too. As you begin the content process, you struggle with things to write about. You can't imagine what anyone would find interesting about your business. But then, you begin to find things: in everyday news, in industry reports, during dinner conversations with friends, or even while you're driving home from work.

You become obsessed with new and interesting ways to tell your story, it seeps into your dreams. It becomes a disease—you just *have* to tell the story. You drop everything to write a web page or a blog post or a white paper, or to record a podcast or video. Just like anything else, it gets easier with practice, and soon you're on your way to selling without sex but with the customer, employee, and company stories that really matter to your customers.

Take Your Story from Idea to Concept

Larry Brooks is an author and blogger who tries to help aspiring authors in his daily musings. He very easily breaks down storytelling; in "Beware the Undercooked Story Concept,"[2] he discusses how to take your story from an idea to a concept. He uses *The Help* as an example of how you could do the same for your organization.

He says, "An 'idea' is *not* inherently a concept. Not until it *transcends* the simplicity of a singular arena or theme or character, and moves toward the unspooling of conflict-driven dramatic tension."

"Too often the writer answers this instead: 'What is your story *about*?' That's not necessarily a concept, either. Let's look at a bestseller to help (no pun) illustrate."

"What is *The Help* about?

- **Three African-American maids in the south.** Yes, it is *about* that. But is that a *concept*? No. It's an *idea*. A starting point. Could go anywhere. And that's the problem…when a writer begins with something this vague, it often does go anywhere, several places, either at once or in sequence…and the story ends up being about some combination of nothing and everything. Such stories become an episodic *The Adventures of So-And-So*, which, like any other story, *isn't* an effective novel until *it* becomes much more conceptual.

- **Racial prejudice in the South.** Yes, it is. But is that a concept? No. Not yet. This is more *theme* than concept. Could be anything, most likely a series of un-connected *stuff* happening to the characters.

- **A book project between a young and wealthy writer that requires the partic-ipation of the black maids being oppressed by their white employers in 1962 Jackson, Mississippi.** Now *this* is a concept. Because it describes more than what the story is about, it opens the door to a dramatic question."

---

2. http://storyfix.com/beware-the-under-cooked-story-concept

"Notice how the first two answers—an idea and a theme—do *not* pose a dramatic question. And that the much stronger answer, the one that really *is* a concept, does."

A good exercise for you to do right now is to put this book down and try this with your organization. Take your vision or mission and use that as the idea, then write the theme just as Brooks describes it, and finally the concept. It won't be fully baked the first time you do it, but you'll see it unfold after you get it on paper and begin to think about it.

Develop Company Characters

Now that you have your idea turned theme turned concept, it's time to begin writing your story. Think of the issues your audience really cares about, your protagonist and antagonist, the revelation, and the transformation.

There are five essential parts to your organization's story: passion, a protagonist, an antagonist, a revelation, and a transformation.

Passion. What is it your audience really cares about? We talked about how MailChimp tells their customers' stories in interesting ways. They don't have their customers talk about how they use MailChimp. They have them talk about their restaurant or their fashion design company or their business cartoons. These aren't customer quotes or testimonials; these are customer stories.

The passion lies in how your product is created, your office culture, the one thing your organization truly cares about that makes you unique and valuable to the world around you.

In Chicago, sports is a big deal, with two major league baseball teams, an NBA team, an NFL team, and myriad other sports teams. Heck, it's a big deal for the entire city. The Bears and Cubs notwithstanding, the Bulls haven't done much lately in the way of getting fans excited until one Derrick Rose came to town. Adidas took notice of the up-and-comer and made the investment: an estimated 13-year, $184 million contract.

Just two weeks later (and early far enough in the playoffs to ruin the chance of a title), Rose tore his ACL, putting him on the bench for a minimum of nine months. Adidas had a new shoe—the D Rose 3.0—launch forthcoming, so they couldn't create a typical superhuman athlete like they might have in the past.

They had to figure out what the audience really cares about. Do they care about the shoes? Probably not. Do they care about Derrick Rose? Perhaps. If they're basketball fans, they might respect him, but they probably don't care about him unless they're Bulls fans. They do care about a superstar turned mortal man and his road to recovery. They do care about the fall from stardom and rebuilding a big career.

His story is an incredible one to begin with—not unlike a major movie script. He's from Chicago, his older brothers taught him how to play basketball, he played for a year at the University of Memphis before he joined the NBA draft, he won rookie of the year, All-Star second year, MVP third year, and then he tore his ACL. There was a scandal involving NCAA violations while he was at Memphis, which provides the fall from grace and the rebuild of his story. And now it needs a happy ending, one in which Rose comes back from injury and takes his team to the championships to win. But the ending is yet to be seen.

Now, not all of you will have $185 million to spend on a spokesperson. Nor will you have the opportunity that Adidas had when Rose tore his ACL. But what Adidas did to tell the story is something any one of you can steal.

They created a documentary series called *The Return*, which they produced and released online. There weren't any big, fancy media buys or three days worth of shooting for one 30-second ad. Rather, they followed Rose during his recovery and used the Web to distribute the story to people around the globe. Rose received more than 14 million messages of support—and I can guarantee those were not all Chicago fans.

As of this writing, the shoe is just beginning to hit the shelves, so whether or not the campaign worked to increase sales hasn't been reported. But what Adidas has released are the soft metrics:

- "Return of D Rose" has been a national trending topic on Twitter three times.

- Twitter followers for @adidasbasketball have increased 100 percent.

- Facebook chatter jumped 200 percent.

- The YouTube videos have been viewed seven million times.

- Online searches for "D Rose 3" increased by 400 percent.

- An estimated 140 million consumers (not including each of you who are reading this) have seen the overall initiative.

They created passion. It was their plan B, and they crushed it. This is an example of thinking quickly on their feet—they had a few weeks (if not days) to come up with something that took advantage of their multimillion dollar investment while he sat on the bench. Another company, however, had mere seconds to figure out what to do next.

Super Bowl XLVII may be remembered for a few things. A highly anticipated halftime show by Beyoncé. Rumors about whether or not Destiny's Child would show up to perform. Wondering if Beyoncé's husband, Jay-Z, would also take the stage. A 108-yard return by the Baltimore Ravens' Jacoby Jones. But most will remember it because the lights went out at the Superdome in New Orleans. Literally.

During those 34 minutes of "downtime," the social networks were alive with jokes: "We've all had a blackout situation in New Orleans!" and "This is a perfect example of how the Clapper is not a good idea for stadium lighting."

And then it happened. The most brilliant move by a company in real time we had yet to experience. Oreo took the stage when they tweeted, "Power out? No problem."

Which was accompanied by a black and white photo (Figure 1.3) with the tagline, "You can still dunk in the dark."

The company did pay an estimated $4 million for a 30-second ad during the game, but when the lights went out, they seized the unanticipated chance to get the name out there again. They were the first advertiser to tweet a response…in less than four minutes.

Figure 1.3 *Oreo capitalizes on a power failure at a major U.S. sports event.*

Being passionate about your organization's story, finding a chance like Oreo did, and telling your story is not just for those who spend millions of dollars on athlete spokespersons or Super Bowl television ads. The advantage Oreo had? Their creative team were all sitting in one room watching the game and monitoring the social networks for mentions of the brand.

They were able to show off their quick thinking and creative storytelling a few weeks later during the Grammys. When Justin Timberlake took the stage, they tweeted "Bringing tasty back" with an image of a bow tie on the cream inside the cookie (Figure 1.4).

Brilliant, brilliant storytelling that doesn't require an expensive media buy or a multi-person creative team. It simply requires that you constantly think about the story you have to tell so you can quickly tie into the current events or industry trends as they're happening. Not four days later, but as they happen. It also requires an engaged community—either through your company blog or on the social networks (more on that in Chapter 9).

How can you tell your story to create passion among the people who will buy your products or services? How can you create an advantage, like Oreo had, by thinking that quickly on your feet?

Figure 1.4   *Oreo continued its Twitter creativity during the 2013 Grammy Awards.*

It doesn't matter what you sell. An oxidizer manufacturing company creates passion around understanding EPA regulations and how they affect air pollution control. A PR firm creates passion around technologic advances. An accounting firm creates passion around accountants with personality. Passion is the first step in telling your story in an engaging and valuable way.

Protagonist. Now that you have your idea, theme, concept, and passion, it's time to create your protagonist. This one is easy. The protagonist is you, your company, your product, or your service. This is typically where stories begin and end—but in our process, this is just the beginning.

To figure out who your protagonist is—the leader of the organization, a social media rockstar within your ranks, a spokesperson, a cartoon superhero of your logo—ask a handful of people in various roles to share five adjectives they'd use to describe the company and two aspects of the organization that are unique or valuable. Ask people inside your organization and your customers to contribute. Look for themes or strong responses and combine them into a clearly defined description of your protagonist's attributes.

For U.K. maxi-pad brand Bodyform, the protagonist was an actress who posed as the company's CEO when a man named Richard Neill went on the attack on their Facebook page.

"Hi, as a man I must ask why you have lied to us for all these years. As a child, I watched your advertisements with interest as to how at this wonderful time of the month the female gets to enjoy so many things. I felt a little jealous. I mean bike riding, roller coasters, dancing, parachuting, why couldn't I get to enjoy this time of joy and 'blue water' and wings!! [. . .] Then I got a girlfriend, was so happy and couldn't wait for this joyous adventurous time of the month to happen…you lied!! There was no joy, no extreme sports, no blue water spilling over wings and no rocking soundtrack oh no no no. Instead I had to fight against every male urge, I had to resist screaming wooaaahhhhhh boddddyyyyyfoooorrrmmm bodyformed for youuuuuuu as my lady changed from the loving, gentle, normal skin colored lady to the little girl from the exorcists with added venom and extra 360 head spin. Thanks for setting me up for a fall bodyform [sic], you crafty bugger."

The company responded a couple days later by hiring an actress to play the CEO in a video.[3] It begins with her sitting at her desk where she pours herself a glass of blue water. She looks straight into the camera, says hello to Richard, introduces herself. She says they read his Facebook post with interest, but also with a sense of foreboding.

She says, "I think it's time we came clean. We lied to you, Richard, and I want to say sorry. Sorry."

She then gets up from her desk and walks over to a flip chart to show images as she talks about how, in the 1980s, they conducted focus groups to see how the public would respond to the harsh reality of periods—the cramps, the mood swings, the insatiable hunger, and, yes, even the "blood coursing through our uteri like a crimson landslide." They decided it was better to change their strategy and, from that day on, they were able to keep up the illusion.

"But you, Richard," she says. "You have torn down that veil and exposed this myth, thereby exposing every man to a reality we hoped they'd never have to face. You did that, Richard. You. Well done."

She ends the video back at her desk, where she picks up the glass of blue water and drinks it.

This is a protagonist. Someone you can believe in. Someone who comes back with a clever response and has a sense of humor. The only thing that could have been done differently would be to put the real CEO in front of the camera instead of an actress. But even without the actual CEO speaking to Richard, you feel a sense of camaraderie with the company and want them to succeed, no matter what challenges they face.

Who is the protagonist in your organization? As soon as you figure that out, you have passion and you have someone people can believe in. Now you need someone—or something—for people to hate…the antagonist.

Antagonist. The antagonist is the villain and often the most overlooked part of an organization's story. What is the enemy of your success? Think about it as an issue or challenge you solve. What keeps your customers awake at night? Is it a cultural issue? Is it an industry concern? Perhaps you work in print distribution and the products you make are becoming extinct because everything is going online and you no longer have something to distribute. Maybe it's a real problem like the hassle of setting up payroll, or you have email overload.

---

3. www.youtube.com/watch?v=Bpy75q2DDow

Chicago-based 37 Signals discovered there was a problem for small- and medium-sized businesses in using customer relationship and project management software: what existed was far too expensive and built only for very large companies. They also knew the Web should empower, not frustrate.

Their antagonist, then, became the big enterprise software solutions for both customer relationships and project management. But it also became the frustrating parts about using the Web—the costly servers, the tricky installations, the 24/7 technical support, and the slow and limited programming languages.

When Basecamp was released in February 2004, the company expected to generate sales of $5,000 per month by the end of the first year. They reached that target in six weeks. They credit much of their success to their creation of tools that are simple and easy to use: the antithesis of everything corporate, costly, and tricky.

Their antagonist is still alive today as they write and rewrite code that creates a better customer experience—one that is simple, easy-to-use, and affordable.

Similarly, ZenPayroll set out to solve the extremely painful process of setting up and managing payroll. There are six million businesses in the United States that still process payroll manually because large companies such as ADP and Paychex are far too expensive—and cumbersome—for a small business.

They set out to get rid of the unnecessary layers of complexity, manual tasks, and numerous fees. Their antagonists, then, are the big vendors in the corporate payroll software space.

What problem do you solve for your customers? Is there a big, bad competitor in your industry? Find your enemy—the antagonist for this part of your story.

The revelation. Part of what makes fiction so compelling are twists or turns you weren't expecting. We enjoy the surprise and delight, even if the revelation is sad, because we like the feeling of being let in on a secret. Your organization's story should share something unexpected with customers and prospects.

There is an interesting company called FoldIt that creates games as a way to solve real issues, such as the design of antiretroviral drugs for AIDS patients. The company is billed as online gaming, but its big revelation is that the games serve the purpose of finding a needle in a haystack—something scientists may miss by not being able to see the forest for the trees.

A game called EteRNA allows lay people to help scientists discover new things. For instance, tutorials in EteRNA teach players the basics of "RNA folding," and they are asked to solve hundreds of practice challenges. After they complete the practice, they're allowed to go into a virtual lab where they are challenged to design molecules. The players vote on one another's designs, based on which ones are most likely to succeed. The top designs are then studied in a Stanford lab.

The company has 30,000 players of all ages worldwide. You may think you're playing a game, but the revelation is that your work could lead to new ways to control living cells and cure diseases.

Green Mountain Coffee Roasters use revelation in their storytelling by actually saying, "There is a revelation in every cup." That means they leave the story up to you as you enjoy your first cup every morning.

They say, "We realize the power of a good cup of coffee. More than just something to drink, it connects us to each other and to the rest of the world. Join us as we explore those connections and the surprising, rich, complex story of coffee. How and where it's grown, the many ways it can be prepared, and the artistry involved along the way. A revelation in every cup."

From there, they take you on a journey to meet the people who have helped transform the coffee experience into one meaningful to you. Their employees tell the story and the revelation becomes about you and your story. What are you going to do that day? How are you going to change your part of the world? Which one of life's paths are you going to traverse? The story becomes about you, the customer, which allows the company to share something unexpected with you in a very personal way.

They also wrap the rest of storytelling into that one paragraph. The passion is around making the very best cup of coffee, the protagonist is the employees, the antagonist is the big, bad coffee roasters who get their beans in unethical ways, the revelation is your own story, and the transformation? Well, that comes next.

Transformation. The final part to your story is the transformation—the thing or things that is different about the way you do business. Think about how your company has evolved. Think about the problem you solve and how it connects with both emotional and practical needs. What is your value proposition? What can customers get only from you? It might be intellectual property, or a new way of doing things, or a super-duper-cool new widget. People want to know how you arrived there.

The argument many business leaders make at this point is, "Why would I want to give away our secret sauce? Then our competitors would do what we do." Here's the thing: Your competitors may know the exact recipe to your secret sauce, but no one does it as well as you do. It's *your* secret sauce. It was created with your people, your thinking, your culture, your passion, and your vision.

Take McDonald's, for instance. In July 2012, their executive chef shared the Big Mac special sauce. Literally shared the exact recipe for the special sauce. You know, the one in the classic jingle, "Two all-beef patties, special sauce, lettuce, cheese, pickles, onions on a sesame seed bun." *That* special sauce.

If you have mayonnaise, sweet pickle relish, yellow mustard, white wine vinegar, garlic powder, onion powder, and paprika at home, you can make the special sauce. The only exception is that at McDonald's, they have to include xanthan gum to thicken it, and potassium sorbate and calcium disodium to preserve it.

But try it at home. Put it on your burgers next time you grill at home. Does it taste the same? Is it even remotely the same? It's the *exact* recipe, yet it tastes nothing like McDonald's.

Ask Wendy's how that turned out for them. They launched the W Burger, which they say has the same Thousand Island dressing on it as their competitor to the Big Mac (check out the ingredients: they're the same as the McDonald's special sauce). They also released the Hot 'n Juicy as their In-n-Out competitor. Just do a search for Wendy's burgers, and you'll find more negative than positive opinions about the taste of both burgers. It's a perfect example of why giving away the recipe to your secret sauce is never a brand killer. Your competitors will fall all over themselves trying to reproduce what you have—while you focus on innovation and new products or services. You'll always be the leader in your space.

There is yet another way you can tell the transformation part of your story.

When Facebook launched Timeline for businesses in March of 2012, people were up in arms about what the changes meant for the brand pages they'd spent so much time caring for and cultivating.

But the *New York Times* quickly took advantage of the new feature and began to tell their story of more than 150 years by way of photos. If you go to their page and click on Founded in the Timeline, it scrolls you all the way back to 1851 where you see an image of the front page of their very first issue (Figure 1.5).

Figure 1.5   *Headline from the first issue of the* New York Daily Times.

The headline reads, "'We publish today the first issue of the New-York Daily Times, and we intend to issue it every morning (Sundays excepted) for an indefinite number of years to come,' wrote *The Times*'s founders, Henry Jarvis Raymond, speaker of the

New York State Assembly, and George Jones, an Albany banker, in the inaugural edition. It cost one cent per copy."

If you click on the 1960s in the Timeline, you'll see photos of the Apollo 11 landing, journalists waiting for word of Senator Robert Kennedy's condition after he was shot in Los Angeles, and the civil rights rally where Martin Luther King, Jr. gave his "I Have a Dream" speech.

Of course, not every company is more than 150 years old or has the rich content the *New York Times* has, but you do have a history. Tell the story of how you got to where you are today. It doesn't have to be in chronological order, but it does have to be interesting.

There is a company in Atlanta that makes faucets. When they tell their story, they do so by showing a photo of their very first location, which was a one-level brick building with four rooms. Then they give you a photo of their showroom now: a 20,000 square foot, gorgeous open space with high-end kitchen and bathroom accessories attached to beautiful appliances and sinks and showers and tubs. Then they show the trade ads they used in the early days, next to the consumer ads they now place in magazines such as *Architectural Digest* and *Home Beautiful*. You see the transformation of their company in a very visual way. It makes you want to do business with them—they bring you into their story without making you feel like they're selling to you.

If you're just starting out, your transformation, from a company perspective, likely hasn't happened yet—but there is a reason you're launching a new business. Maybe it's to provide apps to all musicians, like Foursixty; or to teach people how to run political campaigns, like GetElected. Whatever it happens to be, the transformation is the closing to your story; it's also the part that continues to evolve. So don't get hung up on getting it perfect. If your organization is anything like mine, it could change as quickly as next week.

Now that you have your idea, your theme, your concept, and your story complete with passion, a protagonist, an antagonist, a revelation, and a transformation, you're ready to get out there and tell it.

2

The Google Drama

As you think about how to tell your story, it's important to understand how the search engines—particularly Google—work. As of this writing, Google prioritizes fresh, educational, and valuable new content when crawling your website. Then it looks at things such as social media and links from high-authority sites. This means your website should be consistently updated if you want to rank high in search results. Telling your organization's story as it unfolds is one way to do that.

A bit of a history lesson will help you understand how this works.

When Google launched in 1998, the company's focus was on returning relevant results for users' search queries. Throughout the years, people figured out how to game the system, and search firms began to pop up around the world. They worked to help you achieve better search ranking by tweaking the hidden parts of your website—meta descriptions, meta tags, and back links.

For a long time, these things, if done well, launched your website to the top of search results, which was exciting. But unless you understood how a website was built and how the Google algorithms worked, it felt like magic. And it was a sort of magic. Terms such as "black hat" and "white hat" were thrown around, and business leaders struggled to understand how to hire the right experts so their sites could rise in search results, yet do so in a lawful way—so they didn't end up blacklisted by Google. The joke was that everyone was a search expert, but no one really understood how it all worked.

"White hat" refers to experts who abide by the rules. They understand what the search engines want to accomplish, they keep up with the latest changes, and they use hard work and many, many hours to increase search rankings for the website(s) they manage. White hat professionals have always believed good quality content is the way to achieve good results. They believe in the marathon versus sprint philosophy: It takes time to cross the finish line. They strictly adhere to the SEO Code of Ethics and know how to build sites that are relevant to both humans and search engines.

"Black hat" refers to those who believe the search engines are the enemy. They get a thrill from gaming the system. They live on the edge and don't mind if one of their sites is blacklisted because they have several others to publish as soon as that happens. They will do things such as write nonsensical content littered with search-friendly keywords and phrases. They also have no qualms about stealing content from other sites (known online as scraping—but it's plain old plagiarism) to get the quickest ranking they can. When the search engines ban those sites, they just move on to the next thing.

"Gray hat" refers to those who walk the line between the SEO Code of Ethics and using some black hat techniques. They tend to be more acceptable to the search engines because they stay closer to white hat tactics and don't stray too far into gaming the system. Some of the tactics they use include buying links from sites, particularly online directories, and having duplicate content on pages within their site. For some of these tactics your site can be penalized, but it won't be completely blacklisted. Most search engine optimization experts use some gray hat techniques to help improve the search rankings immediately while they work on the longer-lasting white hat projects.

Today, it's not up to the search engine optimization experts to understand all this. It's up to you. Sure, you might not be able to keep up with all of the changes at Google or understand how those changes affect your website. But you *can* make sure the tactics your team is using are white hat. If you are creating good, valuable, high-quality content, you can rest assured you're doing things the right way. If, however, you're thinking about paying for links or keywords, or duplicating content, exercise caution. While some of that still works, it's becoming increasingly unreliable.

Along Came Panda

In January 2013, Google released its 24th version of Panda. The first version was launched in February 2011, which means there is a refresh nearly once a month. Having to keep up with the Google changes is close to impossible . . . unless it's what you do for a living.

What Google continues to do with its Panda updates is bring back the best search results highlighting the most unique and valuable content. Let's say, for instance, you read an article in the *New York Times* about underwater basket weaving. It's a really well-researched article, complete with interviews and facts never before revealed about underwater basket weaving.

Now, suppose you sell materials people can use to weave their own baskets underwater. It makes sense, then, to use the article in your own marketing. But you can't just copy and distribute it in your offline marketing—that violates copyright laws. And if you copy and paste the article into your website or blog, that will violate the Google Panda rules and they'll blacklist your site more quickly than you can say, "Google Panda."

So what do you do?

You can share your own thoughts on it and quote portions of the article to support your thinking. It's totally acceptable to use quotes from the article in your own content. Don't forget to link to the original article and use quotation marks around what you're copying from it. But the rest of the blog post or article you're writing has to be your own. You can't put quotation marks around the entire article and use it as your own.

After you publish your new and interesting content, Google indexes your site as an authority on underwater basket weaving. When people search for that topic, the *New York Times* article comes up first in search results because they're more authoritative than you, but you come up second. Now anyone searching on the topic has two different articles to read to get smart about their underwater basket weaving. The *New York Times* presents only the news; by writing your own content on the subject, you are exposing readers to the underwater basket weaving products you sell. Now you've made them smart *and* you've sold them products to take with them on their next diving trip to the Cayman Islands.

In February 2006, Matt Cutts, the head of the webspam team at Google, wrote a blog post to explain why the search company was blacklisting the German sites of BMW and Ricoh. These aren't small companies no one has ever heard of; being blacklisted can happen to anyone.

The reason was that both companies violated the Google rules for duplicate content in other languages. They had the same content on those sites as their English sites, but in German. It was not different content. It was just a different language. Google views straight translations as duplicate content and, under their Panda algorithm, they will blacklist you for this.

If you do business internationally and have separate sites for each country, you must have different content. Just having it in a different language will not suffice.

Of course, the BMW and Ricoh German sites were reinstated after they changed their content, but it clearly shows that Google doesn't mess around.

And Then Came Penguin

Between the early 2000s and 2012, search firms made their living on keyword stuffing and backlink strategies that didn't always have anything to do with the website, the products sold, or the services provided.

Let's say your business makes USB drives. The margin isn't very high, the industry is competitive, and the product is a true commodity. To make any money, you have to sell in big bulk, and to win at the web game, you have to spend thousands of dollars every month on Google AdWords. But along comes a search firm who tells you they can get you on the first page of Google for a fraction of what you're paying for AdWords. Seems like a no-brainer.

At first, the firm is extremely successful. You begin to rank for all sorts of competitive phrases, including "USB drives," "USB flash drives," and any combination of storage (4G, 8G, 16G, and so on) when used with one of your key phrases. They're totally rocking it, and you're happy to write that check every month.

Until another black and white animal entered your life. Penguin, a Google algorithm update, was announced in April 2012. Suddenly you don't rank on any search results; in fact, you can't find your site even if you type in your exact company name. You call the search firm. You're extremely upset. They throw up their hands and say, "You can't blame us. Google changed their rules. There is nothing we can do about it."

As you begin to dissect your site, you discover that the search firm did some extremely unethical black hat things. They paid other sites to link to you, and they stuffed your site full of keywords having nothing to do with your business.

Take this example Cutts used in a blog post.[1] A company that promises immortality if you wear their "eternal life rings" got upset with Google for banning their site from search rankings. They say, "Close to 50 percent of people use Google search engine. And for some reason, AlexChiu.com is banned by Google." They claim it's because Google believes their product will eventually put the search engine out of business.

It's a funny example of what happens on the Web, but it's serious business. When Cutts and his team looked at the site, they found irrelevant keyword stuffing. They've circled two specific key phrases Alex Chiu uses (Figure 2.1). What does "plasma tv advanced chart" have to do with immortality? As you scroll through the rest of the keywords, you can see they have nothing to do with staying forever young.

That was why the site was banned from search results, not because Google thought Alex Chiu was a threat to its business.

To go back to the USB drive company example, perhaps the content on your home page reads like this: "Are you looking for cheap USB drives? If you're looking for cheap USB drives, look no further. Our cheap USB drives website is the best place to order your cheap USB drives. Feel free to check out our selection of cheap USB drives from our cheap USB drives selection below."

Do you feel dirty after reading that? Content that reads like this uses keyword stuffing. When we're taught how to write for business in college, our English professors liked to emphasize: "Don't use the same word twice in one sentence." The same goes for website content. If you use the same word or phrase multiple times in a sentence or paragraph, not only will your content be unreadable, but the search engines will penalize your site.

Polaris Public Relations, Inc., a firm in Toronto, had their site penalized and then banned. In 2006, they hired a firm to help with search engine optimization. While

---

1. www.mattcutts.com/blog/avoid-keyword-stuffing

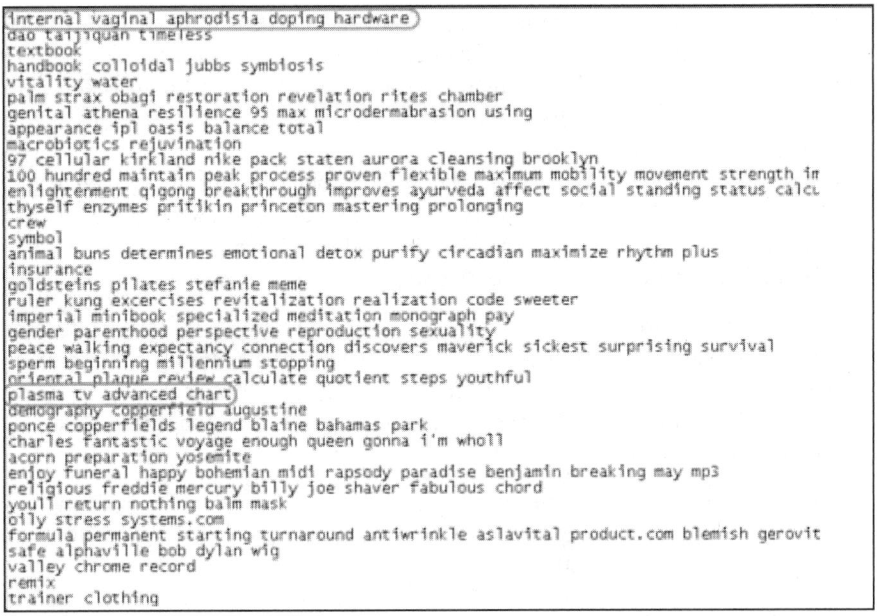

```
internal vaginal aphrodisia doping hardware)
dao taijiquan timeless
textbook
handbook colloidal jubbs symbiosis
vitality water
palm strax obagi restoration revelation rites chamber
genital athena resilience 95 max microdermabrasion using
appearance ipl oasis balance total
macrobiotics rejuvination
97 cellular kirkland nike pack staten aurora cleansing brooklyn
100 hundred maintain peak process proven flexible maximum mobility movement strength in
enlightenment qigong breakthrough improves ayurveda affect social standing status calcu
thyself enzymes pritikin princeton mastering prolonging
crew
symbol
animal buns determines emotional detox purify circadian maximize rhythm plus
insurance
goldsteins pilates stefanie meme
ruler kung excercises revitalization realization code sweeter
imperial minibook specialized meditation monograph pay
gender parenthood perspective reproduction sexuality
peace walking expectancy connection discovers maverick sickest surprising survival
sperm beginning millennium stopping
oriental plague review calculate quotient steps youthful
plasma tv advanced chart)
demography copperfield augustine
ponce copperfields legend blaine bahamas park
charles fantastic voyage enough queen gonna i'm wholl
acorn preparation yosemite
enjoy funeral happy bohemian midi rapsody paradise benjamin breaking may mp3
religious freddie mercury billy joe shaver fabulous chord
youll return nothing balm mask
oily stress systems.com
formula permanent starting turnaround antiwrinkle aslavital product.com blemish gerovit
safe alphaville bob dylan wig
valley chrome record
remix
trainer clothing
```

Figure 2.1 *An example of keyword stuffing used in a website using black hat techniques.*

they weren't reliant on doing business online, founder Shelley Pringle knew it was important to come up in search terms for queries like "Toronto PR firm," "PR Toronto," "PR firms in Toronto," and "public relations Toronto."

According to Pringle, the firm did an excellent job. Polaris began to rank on the first page of search results for all of their keywords. Not only did it help with brand awareness, the business—accustomed to gaining new clients from referrals and word-of-mouth only—began to grow because of prospects finding them on the Web.

And then came Penguin.

In April 2012, the Polaris website disappeared completely from search results. Although the business didn't rely on the Web for growth, it was still devastating. Pringle said the search firm she used had a really good reputation, so she trusted them. Apparently that was a mistake. She did her research to understand why Polaris could no longer be found on the Web without typing in the exact URL, and what she discovered was that the firm had done keyword stuffing and created backlinks that made no sense at all.

She and her team considered writing to Google to try and get their site reinstated—but she knew that, even if she didn't understand what the search firm was doing, she was ultimately responsible. She decided Google probably wouldn't care. They considered breaking the links by contacting the people who owned the linking sites, but she knew that would be extremely time consuming and the return on the time investment likely wouldn't pay off.

Instead, they decided to put their heads down and start creating more content to earn better links. Instead of blogging once a week, the blog was updated multiple times a week. They tested blogging to their targeted keywords, but discovered the content wasn't interesting for people to read, nor was it fun to write. They changed their strategy, and wrote instead about the types of things that were interesting to them—industry trends, news as it relates to public relations, social media, and inbound marketing—and then added keywords into that copy, when it made sense. They also worked on on-page search engine optimization by making their page titles, headlines, keywords, and URLs more natural to a human reader.

It took a year before the site began to rank again, but because Pringle and her team took a long-view and a strategic approach to their content development, this time it has lasted. The search engine optimization they're using is ethical, relevant, and valuable. No matter what Google does to their algorithms in the future, Polaris will continue to rank in search results.

For the rest of us, however, the old saying—"The nice guy always finishes last"—rings true here. You may not come up first or second or tenth in the search results initially, but you will eventually, and you'll stay there.

Marathon Mentality

In 2001, I trained for and ran my very first marathon. I had just moved to Chicago from Kansas City and didn't know a soul. The people I worked with were great colleagues, but I didn't have a lot in common with them outside of the office. I needed to make friends and I thought the best way to do that was to take up a sport that would require me to spend a lot of time with groups of people.

I joined Chicago Area Runners Association and, every Saturday during our long runs, I made some really good friends. I trained with them for my second and third marathons (and all of the shorter races in between) and even convinced some to switch to cycling with me. When I switched to cycling, I went from running marathons to riding centuries (100 mile bike rides) and doing many other kinds of races, such as criterions, time trials, and even racing on the velodrome track. The training for long races is the same, no matter which sport you compete in. I ride every single day, and those rides lead up to one or two long weekend rides (50 miles or more) and a few races each month.

You can't go out and run a marathon or ride a century without training. I know some people *think* they can, but it's humanly impossible. There has to be some sort of training that builds your body up to be able to withstand the abuse it will take during long-distance races.

Search engine optimization works the very same way. If you want to always be safe from changes Google makes to their algorithms, the *only* way to do it is through really good content.

You need to have a marathon mentality.

You can't just go out and get—and stay—on the first page of Google. It's not possible. Just like there are days I don't want to get out of bed to ride, there are days you won't want to create another piece of content for your site. It might be a blog post, or the weekly newsletter, or a podcast, or a video. Maybe you just come up short on ideas. But you have to do it, or your competitors will have a better day and end up winning the race.

When Duplicate Content Gets You in Trouble

When creating content, the question "How often should I post new content?" almost always comes up. The answer depends on your goals, but from a search engine perspective once a week is sufficient. What you really want to be focused on is consistency, and quality versus quantity. If you want to create one new piece of content each week, choose a day and time and publish it at that time. Week after week. Think about it as a daily, weekly, monthly, or quarterly publication. Which one do you want to be? You can always change your mind later, but if you decide to be a weekly publication, the important thing is to publish at the same time on the same day every week.

Of course, the more you publish, the better your results. Not just search ranking results but lead generation, inbound marketing, thought leadership, brand awareness, and more. On the flip side, the more content you've committed to, the more difficult it is to come up with something new and interesting every time.

That's why so many content creators make the *duplicate content* mistake. Sometimes it's as simple as using web page copy in a blog post, other times it's not realizing that similar content is already on the site (maybe it's old or buried deep).

Duplicate content is a very subtle issue. Unless your entire site is a complete duplicate of another (like the BMW and Ricoh examples), it will rarely get you banned from search results outright, nor will it get your site blacklisted. In fact, you will often see the same blog posts running on multiple sites, which if done the right way is considered syndication and not duplicate content.

What should concern you is when you have pages duplicated across your website because of a change in your team, technical issues, or just plain old laziness (which *should* create a change in your team!). The search engines will not immediately penalize you if this happens. But it does mean you should get to work to change those pages. Consider them a small fire burning in a trashcan. You want to put it out, but it's not going to spread if you walk to the kitchen to look for your fire extinguisher, or to grab a bucket of water.

That said, if you are doing things well, content scrapers will steal your content and run it on their own sites. This is where you need to be concerned. A few simple steps will help you find where your content is being reproduced without permission.

The first is to set up Talkwalker Alerts for your company name, your products or services, and/or your blog name. When someone mentions your search terms online, you'll receive an email. Always link to another page on your website or blog when publishing new content. This creates what's called a trackback, so if anyone scrapes that content, they'll pick the link as well, and the trackback will show you where it's appearing. For most of you, this is something your content team should do, but you should be knowledgeable on the topic so you can ask the right questions.

If someone has scraped your content, you have a few options. An easy—and effective—tack is to comment on the article and ask them to take it down. If they don't, you can try reporting them to the search engines. Usually you can let it go with commenting on their site because now you know they know you are on to them. And, if you're taking the long-view, marathon approach to content, your website or blog will have much higher authority than any site that scrapes your content. You'll appear first in search rankings anyway.

If you're just starting out and haven't yet created authority in the eyes of the search engines, it's important to pay close attention to where your content is being reused or scraped. It won't happen overnight, but you'll see a sharp increase fairly quickly as you begin to develop new content, and higher authority. If someone steals your content, you want to report it. While the site won't be penalized immediately, the search engines will eventually list it as a spammy, low-quality website and eventually penalize its rankings. So your content will show up in search rankings—and theirs will not.

Here's another duplicate content consideration: Let's say you have two pages on your site with the same title—though one is written in singular ("heat recovery system") and the other in plural ("heat recovery systems"). The URLs may be different, but the copy on the two pages is exactly the same. Google will strike both of those pages out of its search results and lower the site's overall rankings.

It used to be common practice to do for websites, because people search both ways. The web firm would create two pages so your site would appear in either search—but the same content was used on both pages. This no longer works. You need to go through your website (or have someone on your team go through it) to make sure there isn't any duplicate content anywhere.

That said, you don't want to get rid of the singular and plural pages altogether. Instead, change the copy on one of the pages. It won't be easy—heat recovery system and heat recovery systems are the same thing, after all—but you likely can repurpose copy from other places, such as your company brochures, print ads, or white papers that live as PDFs on the site but don't have their own pages.

We'll talk more about how to manage content farms and illegal reproduction of your content in Chapter 6. For now, set up your Talkwalker Alerts and make sure every piece of new content you produce for your website hyperlinks to another page on your site or blog that is relevant to the piece you just wrote.

The best course of action is to create high-quality content that hasn't been replicated anywhere on your site or blog. This is the best way to prevent any penalties from the search engines as their algorithms continue to evolve.

What Constitutes High-Quality Content?

If you're having trouble, there are questions you can ask yourself to help. These questions will serve as your guide during the rough days. As you work through the list, ask yourself one very important question: Why is it that we all hate spam, self-serving newsletters, and the "me, me, me" found on most websites—but when we get to work and sit at our desks, we create the exact stuff that drives us crazy personally? Maybe it's because our bosses want it that way or, if you are the boss, you don't know of any other way to do it. After all, people do it, so it must work, right?

No! It doesn't work. And Google will not love you if you continue this practice.

As you're creating your content—blog posts, articles, website copy, e-books, white papers, newsletters, podcasts, videos, brochures, case studies—ask yourself the following questions, suggested by the search engine's guidelines:

- If you received the information presented in the article, blog post, or email, would you trust it?

- Is this something you would bookmark and share with your friends, peers, and colleagues?

- Is the content written by an expert inside your organization, or is it written by someone without any experience or expertise?

- Do you respect the author's opinion—even if you disagree with it?

- Does your site have content that is similar? If so, is the new content so similar that Google won't be able to tell the difference?

- Has the content been edited? Is it free of typos and spelling and grammatical errors? Is it factually correct?

- Is the topic interesting to your customers and prospects? Does it help them better understand how to use your product? Are you giving them something to help them in their jobs? Are you making their lives easier?

- Does the content provide original thinking? Even if you are using something in the news to tie back to what you do, does it have your own opinion included?

- Have you done a search for your topic or keywords? Does your content provide substantial value when compared with the content that comes up in search results?

- Is your site recognized as an authority on the topic?

- Is the content solely yours?

- Does the content provide a complete description of the topic?

- Does the content provide insight, analysis, or other interesting information that is different than what others are producing?

- Would you expect to see this content in an encyclopedia, magazine, or book?

- Is it easy to read, with subheads, bullet points, or lists to help people easily scan?

A good rule of thumb is: If you don't want to bookmark it and share it, no one else will, either.

The biggest challenge with ethical and valuable content creation is simple ignorance: Many of us don't know how to do it, so it's easy to slip into just getting it "done" and off your task list. While this wouldn't have hurt you in the past, it will now.

Yes, it is harder to produce interesting and valuable content. But, much like marathon training, it pays off in the end. Sure, you may hit the proverbial wall, but if you push through it and your competitor does not, you'll win every time.

3

Shareable and Valuable Content Creation

In 2011, the Public Relations Society of America (PRSA) set out to redefine public relations. An honorable cause: The industry's premier trade association felt it was time to help business leaders understand what it is we do. After all, the last time it was defined was in 1982.

In fact, for more than 70 years, public relations was done the exact same way. The only tangible result coming from our desks were stories written or produced on behalf of the companies for which we work. Sure, there is a lot more to what we do—crisis and reputation management, events, messaging, employee relations, financial reporting, and brand building, to name a few—but the only thing you could hold in your hand and touch and feel was a story in a business journal, a trade publication, or a newspaper or magazine.

For those of us in the industry before 2008, a majority of time was spent building relationships with journalists. The successful befriending of a business columnist for *USA Today* was a relationship carefully cultivated. For years, if a client made sense to a journalist's column requirements, he could source that organization or its executives for quotes or commentary for many stories, using one PR professional or firm. But, let's say in 2008, that same columnist was forced to take mandatory furlough from the paper, never to be reinstated. Suddenly, those years spent building a relationship with such an influential journalist went down the drain.

That was the beginning of a very interesting trend: The PR industry was turned on its head as newspaper after newspaper and popular magazine after popular magazine quietly folded, turning their journalists out into the big, scary world of unemployment.

It was a good shock for the industry. Now, we're moving toward more innovative and interesting actions, resulting in measurable results for an organization and its goals. Nonetheless, because the industry has always been known as only "media relations," this shift is not moving fast enough.

To this day, if someone calls us out of the blue saying they're looking for a PR firm, the first few questions asked during the phone call are pointed: We want to uncover what they mean by that. Usually, they mean "Get us on the front page of the *New York Times*." If that's the definition of PR to a potential new prospect, they're not a good fit for our organization.

Do you think we're crazy because we turn down business just because it's steeped in the past? Well, we're not. And here's why: There are two new kids in town. One is named *owned media* and the other is *shared media*. And together with their brothers, *paid media* and *earned media*, they're shaking up the PR landscape.

Figure 3.1 demonstrates the chart we use to show business leaders what we do everyday. It also describes the different types of media and the tactics that fall underneath each.

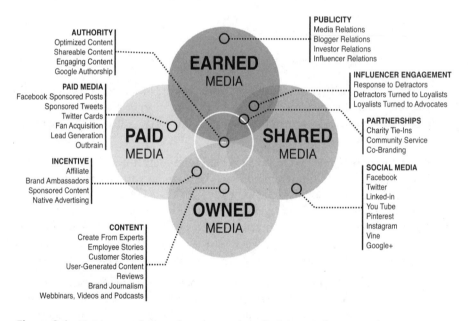

Figure 3.1   *Paid, earned, shared, and owned media integrate for a complete communications program.*

Let's look at the definitions of the four types of media and explore some examples of how they work in the real world.

Paid Media

Paid media is what you know of as advertising. You pay for space in a newspaper or magazine, on a radio or television program, on billboards, on websites, in Google, even in subway stations.

If you're paying to put your message somewhere, it falls in this category. Typically you hire (or have internally) a creative agency that develops your advertising campaign, creates a witty slogan or jingle, and helps you place it in the right places. It's expensive and it's hard to measure, but it's one of the few ways to get your message out to the masses in a very fast and effective way. When integrated with the other three forms of media, paid media can still be one of your most effective tools. For example, if you embed your commercial on your home page and also share it on YouTube, you pull your initial viewership to your site for a second viewing. That means you get twice the play.

A great example of clever advertising is what DirecTV is doing with the Manning brothers called "Football on Your Phone." The goal of the ad, of course, is to encourage prospective customers to buy DirecTV before the start of the football season so you don't miss a single game. You can get the games on your TV, your computer, your tablet, and your phone—no matter where you are or what you're doing. Football on your phone allows you to literally carry the entire NFL season in your pocket.

The ad is shot like a music video. The football stars are wearing really awful 70s wigs and have three women backup singers. Even their dad—Archie Manning—makes an appearance. It's extremely well done, slickly produced, and has millions of views.

It wasn't aired on television. There wasn't an expensive media buy (though the video was probably fairly expensive to produce and shoot). It was shot and uploaded to the DirecTV YouTube channel. They then let shared media take the reins and promote it. In fact, the only place you can find it on their website is by clicking the YouTube icon in the lower left corner of their home page. They used paid (because it cost them to produce it), owned media (it is embedded both on their website and their YouTube channel), and shared media for this campaign, and earned media was the result.

By doing a Google search, you can find nearly half a million news results for the ad. That means nearly half a million blogs, TV stations, newspapers, magazines, and radio stations picked up the ad and embedded it on their sites—without the PR team having to call all of those journalists, bloggers, and producers as part of an earned media campaign.

Think about that for a minute. In the old days, your PR firm or internal team would have had to call every single one of those outlets. Calling half a million places not only wouldn't have been cost effective—it would have taken an entire year. But today, in less than 24 hours of its release, the ad created all that buzz by using only two forms of media really well.

Of course, not all of us have the budgets or cache to be able to hire three NFL superstars and shoot a highly produced music video. And that's okay. Think back to the example of Bodyform in Chapter 1. They responded to a Facebook commenter by shooting a video in a conference room with an actor. What if, instead of hiring an actor, someone in your office—maybe even you—could star in your video?

Today video production isn't as cost prohibitive as it used to be. You may not want to shoot something for your paid media campaign with a smartphone, even though it certainly isn't impossible to do so. Instead, call your local news station and ask if they freelance out their videographers. Many do, and they will make some recommendations on whom you can call. They'll have experience to not only professionally shoot your video, but help you tell a story so compelling people will not only watch it but to share it.

When done well, paid media is an extremely effective way to integrate with the other forms of media and gain long-tail exposure that will help you build your brand, increase your credibility, and sell.

Earned Media

Earned media is what is also known as media relations or publicity. It's getting your story told through the *New York Times* or on *The Today Show*. It's showing up for a guest appearance on the local TV "news at noon" or on the NPR podcast *Wait, Wait . . . Don't Tell Me!* It's writing a letter to the editor, or having an article published with your byline on it.

It's called earned media because you don't pay for it; you earn it through relationships, incredibly newsworthy stories, and targeted messaging.

In the late 90s, PRSA came out with a new way of measuring media relations in a scientific way. When calculating *impressions* and *advertising equivalencies*, you use a formula to figure out how effective your public relations campaigns were, as related to the stories told.

For impressions, if a story ran in one of your targeted trade publications, take their circulation and multiply it by five; the number means if one person subscribes and leaves it on their lobby table, at least four other people will pick it up and read it. Called the pass-along rate, it was two and a half for consumer publications; and since you couldn't (at the time) pass along a television or radio program, their numbers weren't multiplied.

For instance, if you got a story in *Better Homes & Gardens*, its circulation is 378,048, so your impressions were 945,120—implying that's how many people read the story about your organization. Now, we all know nearly one million people did not really read that story, but it was the first time the industry had numbers to prove effectiveness of a campaign, and business leaders began to ask for it. In fact, some still ask for it (although I hope that changes after you finish reading this book) because the numbers look impressive in board meetings or as a way to protect your investment when it comes to budget cuts.

Then we have advertising equivalencies, for which you measure the length and width of the article (or the time spent talking about it on TV or radio) and figure out how much that would have cost had it been an ad. Another silly metric—but at the time it was the only way to show effectiveness. After all, the executive team understands numbers. So, it stuck.

Between impressions and advertising equivalencies, you had a number of people who saw or read your story and you had how much it would have cost had it been an ad, giving you a *return on investment.*

Fast forward to today's digital world where you can track exactly what people are doing (provided you're using earned media tactics on the Web), and suddenly we have a way to measure effectiveness in real numbers that matter to the organization. That said, it's still incredibly difficult to earn a story with an influential blogger, a tweet or two from a Twitter superstar, or three minutes on the local noon news—and measure that against an increase in sales. (Unless, of course, your business model is e-commerce only: then you can track bumps in sales against those things on the day—and time— they ran.)

But you're still earning stories, blog posts, Facebook updates, tweets, podcasts, interviews, and more. In some cases, the traditional influencers—journalists, editors, producers—are the audience; in other cases, new influencers include customers, brand ambassadors, critics, bloggers, and someone with a lot of social network followers. Earning those stories or mentions means you still have no control over what will be said. Sure, you can tell your side of your story, but if the influencer experiences something different, don't try to persuade them not to tell their side.

In February 2013, *New York Times* reporter John Broder took the electric Tesla Model S sedan for a drive along the newly electrified stretch of I-95 on the east coast. The electric car manufacturer, run by Elon Musk, helped put charging points into place at service stations at 200 mile intervals along the freeway.

Broder said in his review about the car, "That is well within the Model S's 265-mile estimated range, as rated by the Environmental Protection Agency, for the version with an 85 kilowatt-hour battery that I drove—and even more comfortably within Tesla's claim of 300 miles of range under ideal conditions. Of course, mileage may vary."

So far, so good. Broder has the information he needs from Tesla. The messaging is accurate, the charging stations are close enough together, and he's ready to take his drive. He goes on to compliment how gorgeous the car is and how much he likes the Google-driven navigation system. He talks about all of the awards the car has won and how much fun he expects it will be to drive. All of this, of course, based on what the car company has told him.

Then he experiences the car himself. He starts off on a nice drive on a 30 degree day and makes it to the first charging station just fine. And then the proverbial wheel comes off. While the car's system says it's fully charged, Broder discovers he's losing charged miles faster than he should, so he slows down, turns off the heat, and drives in the right lane until he gets to the next charging station. Frustrated, he charges and gets to a hotel with some 90 miles of range—about twice the 46 miles he needs to get back to a charging station the next morning.

But when he gets up and goes out to start the car in the now 10 degree weather, he finds the car display shows only 25 miles of remaining range, meaning he won't be able to make it to the charging station. In the end, he needs to have the car towed to the charging station where he waits 80 minutes for it to recharge so he could get back to Manhattan.

This recap is told in an eloquent 2,000 word article that details every moment of the more-than-24-hour test drive. Broder describes how several different Tesla employees—from an agent and product planner to the chief technology officer—helped him during his drive. And then Elon Musk gets involved.

Three days after Broder's article runs, Musk tweets, "NYTimes article about Tesla range in cold is fake. Vehicle logs tell story that he didn't actually charge to max & took a long detour." (See Figure 3.2.)

Elon Musk ✔
@elonmusk

🐦 Follow

NYTimes article about Tesla range in cold is fake. Vehicle logs tell true story that he didn't actually charge to max & took a long detour.

7:26 PM - 11 Feb 13

1,128 RETWEETS 226 FAVORITES

Figure 3.2   *Tesla CEO Elon Musk tweets about* New York Times *article that criticizes his cars.*

Even if he didn't actually charge to the maximum and did take a long detour, as both a Tesla customer and a highly influential journalist, his experience is different from what the company promised. Imagine if Broder had just paid more than $100,000 for the car and had this experience—and then tweeted about it, put it on Facebook, and told his friends not to buy it. Would Musk debate him then?

Unfortunately, the story doesn't end there. Musk continues to tell the world why Broder is wrong, detailing their side of the story on the Tesla blog. Some rabid Tesla fans have come to Musk's aid—but overall, he ends up looking defensive.

This demonstrates both the magic and the challenge of earned media. If your customers and influencers love what you're selling and have the same experience as you've told them to expect, earned media works magically in your favor. It's good for your ego, it's good for business, and it makes people want to buy from you.

But you're also taking a risk, like Tesla did with one of the most powerful newspapers in the world. Broder's experience was different from what Tesla had promised—his expectations were not met and he was sorely disappointed, not to mention completely put out. If Musk had handled it in a humble way, with an apology and a "here's what we learned and what we'll change as we release 20,000 cars this year"—while still showing the data they had collected—this would have been a nonstory.

In Chapter 7, we talk a lot about how you no longer have perceived control of your brand's messaging. The Tesla story goes to show that no matter what you say and do, if your operations and the customer's experience don't match your messaging, no amount of talk will undo that. We talk more about this conundrum in Chapter 9.

Shared Media

Shared media is what we all know as social media. The term has changed to shared because, as the social networks evolve and organizations get more savvy about using the tools, the publicity you gain through a grassroots effort like this becomes a combination of how it's consumed and shared *and* engagement or conversation.

Unfortunately this is not the Field of Dreams: If you build it, they most likely will not come. Many organizations think, "We need a Facebook page!" Or, "Let's get a Twitter account!" And they don't consider why they are doing it, aside from the fact that the competition is doing it. Then, because there isn't a strategy or a reason for using shared media, frustration sets in, time is wasted, and efforts are abandoned.

When the social networks exploded, all of the experts said, "Be conversational. Build a community. Engage your audiences. Network with people around the globe. Be social." All of that still rings true but there is another consideration.

With the Google Panda[1] update, you are now ranked on whether or not people share your content on the social networks.

The search engine wants to see that you consistently create new content and that people want to share it on their networks. Double gold stars if they share it on Google+[2] and if you use video and host it on YouTube.

The biggest mistake a lot of organizations make—experienced and inexperienced—is to not have social share buttons anywhere on their site. These aren't the buttons visitors can click to follow you on the social networks; rather the buttons visitors can click that allow them, with one thumb swipe, to share your content on their social networks.

The first step you need to take is ensuring you have social media share buttons on your site so it's easy for visitors to share your owned media (description following). You also should spend some time building networks of your own.

---

1. www.seo-theory.com/2013/04/10/how-the-google-panda-algorithm-works
2. http://plus.google.com

Don't go out and try to do that on all of the social networks. Studies have shown Facebook is the most effective for consumer-facing businesses and LinkedIn is for those working business-to-business. Choose the one or two networks that best fits your audience (hang out where they already participate) and start there.

If your goal is simply to rank higher in search results, use Google+. While Google hasn't come right out and said you will have better results for your keywords if you use their social network, test after test—for any kind of organization—proves that to be true.

Owned Media

Now let's talk about owned media.

Owned media is a channel you control, and it helps tell your story the way you want it told. All of the content on your website—blogs, white papers, webinars, e-books, case studies, videos, podcasts, newsletters, and more—is yours. You own it. If something happens to one of the social networks, your owned content isn't affected because while it was shared through those social networks, it isn't housed there. You have full control of where that content resides, how it's distributed, and whether it's monetized.

The content you own creates a brand personality, helps extend your network, and brings prospective clients and/or customers to your website, where you can manage the marketing funnel.

There is fully owned content, which is on your website, and partially owned content, which are the updates, images, and videos you put on the social networks. While you still own that content, assuming you use it to bring people back to your website, if something were to happen to one of the social networks, your content would go with it.

There are many organizations—particularly small businesses or startups—that want to use the social networks to build their presence instead of developing their own website.

This is a very bad idea.

Here's why. Facebook will lose relevance. Twitter will die. Something new will come to market and replace the existing social networks. That is simply part of the evolution of digital media—and it's why you should put your content on something you own. Then you can lend it—and your community—to the various social networks.

You should think about it as a circle. You produce the content and publish it to your website or blog, then you distribute it through email and the social networks—which brings people back to your website or blog. That way you can measure it. You can analyze your data. You can make informed decisions on what works and what doesn't. Your content can become fluid as it's tested and retested because you're in control. Where earned media relies on instinct and gut, owned media relies on math and science.

Alright—now you have to think about owned media from a content perspective. It is a lot of work, but it doesn't have to be painful. You likely already have a ton of content that can be repurposed.

The first thing every organization must do is review their website and remove the French (the *we, we we*). The easiest way to do this, while admittedly not a very green option, is to print out the pages of your website and go through each one. Circle all of the "we," "us," and "our." If you have a content management system that allows you to search, find those words and make notes of the copy changes that need to happen. Then rewrite the content so, from the customer's point of view, it becomes about *them*, not you.

Voila! You have new content—new owned media—that you can share on the social networks. Now you want to do an audit of what already exists on your site: white papers, webcasts, videos, images, newsletters, products, old inventory, e-books, case studies, testimonials, collaterals, data sheets, brochures, ads, news releases, articles, infographics, events, research, podcasts, presentations, pricing, interviews, reviews, FAQs, survey data, calculators.

Based on that list alone, it's fairly likely you have a ton of content that can be shared—but also updated and repurposed to help build your owned media. Some of it will take work because you'll have to update or revise it, but it's certainly a lot easier than starting with a blank sheet of paper. You may even want to organize it differently on your site, as now you'll have a better idea of what you have and what you need to create.

For instance, we have a client that has years and years of very smart, very relevant content, but it's hard to find on their website. Working with their internal web team, we created three different buckets: media center, resource center, and blog.

In the media center, there are things such as news releases, the company in the news, awards and recognition, events, company overview, logos, photos, bios, and contacts (social media, email, and phone). The resource center has white papers, commentary, speeches, presentations, videos, and podcasts. And the blog has a lot of long form content, such as that found in the resource center, that has been shortened, made more conversational, changed to first person, and republished.

Each of the pages has social share buttons, which makes it easier for visitors to share their content (and Google loves), and a place for people to comment, ask questions, and brainstorm with other visitors.

The magic is, we didn't have to create new content; we were able to repurpose what they already had. The second phase was to share that content on the social networks in a smart, strategic, and non-self-serving way. It gave the client "new" content for more than a year while we worked on creating new content for the second year.

Once you've taken the French out of your website and done an audit of your existing content, you have a list of what needs to be created in order to help achieve business goals. Perhaps it's to generate new leads or nurture and convert existing leads. Perhaps it's to create an online impulse buy. Or maybe it's to simply build brand awareness for a new product or service. Whatever the goal, you have to be able to measure your efforts back to real results.

The best and most effective way to measure owned media efforts is to provide calls-to-action. What do you want people to do after they've read, listened to, or watched your content? Do you want them to download longer content? Participate in a free trial? Subscribe to your newsletter or blog? Request a meeting or proposal? Hire you or buy your product?

The answer could be yes to all of those questions, or it could be yes to just one or two. Know what it is you need to achieve and use your calls-to-action to help you get there.

Create Calls-to-Action

Let's look at three different examples of building community, generating leads, and driving sales.

Build community. In my office, we have what we call "the Facebook question of the week." A few years ago, one of our smarty pants young professionals said to me, "You travel the world talking to business owners about how they should use video to engage potential buyers, but we're not using it."

Like attorneys and accountants, we sell our brains for a living. Our time equals money. So when someone asks if they can pick our brains, they're essentially asking us for our product for free. We were talking about this during a staff meeting one day, and the idea of creating a video was on all of our minds. Someone said, "Why don't we let people pick our brains through our Facebook page?"

And so the Facebook question of the week was born. The goal was to do nothing more than build community and engage friends, clients, prospects, and competitors. People "pick our brains" by asking a question on our Facebook wall; we answer in a two minute or less video, shot using our computer camera, then we upload to YouTube. The video is embedded onto the home page of our website, in the sidebar of our blog, and is distributed to all of our social networks.

We measure not only how many questions we get, but the number of video views, visitors to those pages on the website and blog, comments, social shares, and new likes we get on our Facebook page. This also makes the person whose question was chosen feel really special and important—they gain 1 minute of their 15 minutes of fame when my entire organization, and all their social connections, are talking about it that day, which leads to creating loyal brand ambassadors for life.

Generate leads. The very best way to generate leads is through content. Think about content with two perspectives: free and paid. Paid content doesn't necessarily mean money is going to exchange hands; rather, you're getting something in exchange for your content, such as an email address or phone number.

Let's say you want to have a free monthly webinar, but people will have to register to attend. This is both a free and paid model. They are paying you with their email address, which means they have given you permission to market to them, and they're getting an informative, free webinar.

But how do you generate leads with one webinar? This is the fun part! You get to use both traditional and new tactics to gain registrations. You'll use media relations, email marketing, social media, direct mail, content, and advertising. In some cases, you'll be marketing the webinar to people you already know, but they could be prospects who haven't made a decision to work with you, former clients, or someone new entirely.

Here's is a list of steps for how you might do this. Of course, this list could change, depending on your business and industry, but it provides a good place to begin thinking about how to generate good, qualified leads from content.

1. Choose a topic and a headline that has great search potential. For instance, we hosted a webinar about Google analytics. Rather than call it "Advanced Analytics," we called it "The Lies and Truths of Google Analytics." This is much more compelling to someone who doesn't know what great content you offer.

2. Set up the webinar with your provider (brightTALK, GoToWebinar, Adobe Connect, and WebEx are some of the favorites) and grab the registration link they provide. You'll include that in the email your participants get after they've registered.

3. Create a landing page on your website or blog (you can use HubSpot, FormStack, Impact, or Landerapp) that requires registrants provide their name, company name, and email address to register and also provides all the information attendees need to know about the webinar.

4. Create a list of tactics you're going to use to distribute information about the webinar: news releases, social networks, email, blog, Facebook ad, Google ad, postcard.

5. Using the URL of the landing page (not the URL of the webinar software registration), create a different link for each of the tactics using the Google URL Builder. What this does is create a campaign in your Google Analytics account under Traffic Sources > Sources > Campaigns. When you open that tab, it will list the visitors per tactic. So you'll have "March 28 Webinar from Newsletter," "March 28 Webinar from Social Media," "March 28 Webinar from News Release," and so on. This gives you data to use for the next month so you know which tactics work best for your audience.

6. Shoot a one-minute video to describe what people will learn in the webinar. You can house this on your website and/or blog, distribute it through the social networks, and use it in email marketing. Human beings are visual creatures. You'll be amazed by how well this one thing works.

7. One month before the webinar, distribute a news release (using your media relations URL in the body) on the wire (PR Newswire, BusinessWire, or Pitch Engine, depending on your budget). Also upload the release to the newsroom on your website.

8. If you have a newsletter, include the webinar in the email one month prior to its date.

9. Now you want to think about email marketing, separate from the newsletter. If you have a newsletter, you'll have three other emails. If you don't, you'll do four emails. Do one a month before, one three weeks before, one a week before, and one the day before. It will seem like a lot to you, but most people get the information and sit on it only to register the day before the event. The URL you use in the emails will be different from what you use in the newsletter so you can track the effectiveness of each.

10. A week before the webinar, you'll want to think about social media efforts, as well as writing a blog post (if you have a blog). Because we have a crazy, fun community at Spin Sucks, it is our most effective marketing tool for webinars. But most of our clients find success in email campaigns. Test, test, test—and measure, measure, measure.

11. Using the social media URL you created, begin to post the webinar on your social networks. Ask your team to do the same. If you have a guest speaker for the webinar, have them share it. If you have a LinkedIn company page, share it there and ask people for recommendations so it rises in search results inside the social network. **Fair warning:** Most registrations do not come from the social networks, so don't expect too much from this tactic.

12. If you have a blog, write a post about what people can expect to learn if they attend. This is not a sales pitch. It's valuable and educational content that motivates people to register. It should talk about what you learned from watching it prepublication and why you're excited to share it with your community.

13. If you want to test Facebook, LinkedIn, Twitter, or Google ads, they're very inexpensive ways to see if you can attract new visitors who don't already know about you and your business. Do this two weeks out.

14. You can also go really old school and send a postcard to your database. Because that's rarely done anymore, it can be pretty effective. Do this a month out and make sure your URL is specific to direct mail so you can track how well it works.

Now it's time for the webinar. Make sure you record it because not everyone will attend live. In fact, a good 50 percent of those who registered won't show up. But that's okey. They have registered and you have their email addresses! After the webinar, send an email to everyone who registered which includes a link to the recording. **Put the recording on your website** so you can track who visits and downloads. You can also put it behind a landing page so that anyone new has to enter their email address to download it.

For the most part, the people who register for your webinar are qualified leads. Some will be competitors because they want to see what you're up to and will want to mimic you, but most will be people who want to do business with you.

At this point, you can decide if you hand those leads over to your sales team or, if you have a lead nurturing program, place them into your system for follow-up content to push them through the marketing funnel to a decision.

Drive sales. Just like the other two calls-to-action defined here, there are many ways to use content to help drive sales. Marcus Sheridan, the founder of River Pools and Spas and author of "The Sales Lion" blog uses an e-book, *Inbound and Content Marketing Made Easy*, as his entree to prospects who want to hire him for consulting. The book is free, and when someone calls, inquiring about his consulting services, he sends them the link.

He then tracks whether or not the person has downloaded the book. If they do, he gives them a few days to start reading it before he follows up. If they don't download it, he knows they're not a qualified lead for him so he doesn't waste his time. This is very scary to do. This story invariably makes someone say, "But what if it is a really good prospect and I've not followed up with them?"

Think about how you buy, particularly if it's something you don't consistently buy. Things such as big-ticket items (cars, computers, cameras, appliances), professional services (lawyers, accountants, PR firms), or gifts. What's the first thing you do? You search online. You read. You do your research. You educate yourself. So if the prospect isn't willing to do the research and educate him or herself, Marcus doesn't take the time to do it for them.

That's just one example of how to use content to drive sales. But what if you sell something that has a long sales cycle, or is expensive, or is purchased only once every 10 years? Then your opportunity for content increases dramatically because you want to be top-of-mind when your prospect is ready to buy. The best way to do that is to continually offer the most valuable content to help prospects begin to trust you, to build kinship, and eventually to drive purchases.

For small businesses, you might not have any customer relationship management software and are tracking everything in Excel. That's okay—as long as your tracking leads somewhere. Of course, this also means you're manually tracking how leads are finding you, what they do once they land on your site, where they go from there, and whether or not they end up buying. The more leads you generate, the harder using Excel or a whiteboard becomes.

A good combination is Salesforce for customer relationship management, Marketo or Infusionsoft for email and marketing automation, and advanced Google Analytics. If your organization can't afford that combination, consider cost-efficient alternatives such as Highrise or MailChimp.

The point here is not to wait until you can afford enterprise-level software, but to use what is available to you now in an effective way. What you want to track is how someone found you. Did they subscribe to your blog or follow you on Twitter? Did they download a white paper, attend a webinar, attend a live Q&A you hosted through Google Hangouts, or did you meet at an event? Knowing that will help you determine the types of content they need next to make a decision. And, when you track where they came from and what they did through the sales cycle, you can begin to pinpoint which types of content work best to drive sales.

Your content isn't just about these three things. You also want to think about:

- Place a call-to-action on every piece of owned media you create. This could be social share buttons, a subscription, or the requirement of an email address for download.

- Create landing pages where people download your content. These help you track the effectiveness of one particular piece of content.

- Offer some piece of content in exchange for their registration data (that is, email address and phone number).

- Build your database: generate leads, nurture those leads with new and interesting content, and convert those leads to customers.

- Bring in your sales team and integrate your efforts with them.

If you're able to create a holistic approach with all of your media efforts (paid, earned, shared, and owned), you'll soon become a hub in a wheel of information. Your communications programs will be an investment with a pretty significant return.

Shareable and Valuable Content

The trend toward using the Web to grow your business continues. Email keeps growing exponentially, with trillions sent every year, Facebook went from university students only in 2004 to more than a billion users eight years later. Pinterest became one of the fastest-growing social networks ever, and billions of videos are streamed on YouTube each day.

But the most alarming stat is the number of blogs created only to be abandoned in favor of Facebook, Tumblr, Twitter, or the newest shiny toy.

This is a very bad idea!

It's not easy to have consistently fresh content that people want to read and share and shout from the rooftops. That's why a content development process is essential. Consider:

1. **Subscribing to SmartBrief.** The SmartBrief newsletters aggregate a bunch of content every day (at least 10 articles) around one topic, such as entrepreneurship, leadership, or social media, that is applicable to something you care about. It's pretty likely they have a newsletter for your industry.

2. **Subscribing to Talkwalker Alerts.** A replacement to Google Alerts, Talkwalker Alerts are even better, provide more relevant results, and are free. Let's say you work in an industry that sells in the automotive aftermarket. You can set up alerts for "automotive aftermarket," "sound solutions + auto industry," and "dash insulators + auto industry." This will give you plenty of really good story ideas just from scanning those every day.

3. **Reading the comments.** If you have an active community on your blog or on one of the social networks, read the comments! You will get story ideas just from what people say—things you hadn't yet considered or different perspectives. But what if no one is commenting on the content you create? Read the comments on other blogs within the industry. Read the Twitter streams. Read the comments on Facebook updates. This is what we'll call real-time research. Find out what strikes the fancy of your audience.

4. **Paying attention to current events.** There is almost always something happening in the news that you can comment on for your industry. You can think about how Livestrong is pulling away from its founder and what that means for other nonprofit organizations. Or it could be how Yahoo! is requiring employees to work in an office and what that means for human resources or culture or leadership. Or it could be leadership lessons from Nelson Mandela. When you begin to read, watch, or listen to current events, you'll find ways to relate it back to your expertise. The more you do it, the more natural it becomes.

5. Going through your sent mail. This is a tip from Andy Crestodina, the co-founder of web development firm, Orbit Media. He suggests you go through your sent mail to see what types of things you've sent to customers, prospects, and vendors that could be used for content. Most of us write emails to explain a sales process, a feature or benefit, or our thinking. Use those emails to publish nonproprietary information online.

Now let's say you've done all that and you're still coming up empty. Or you're sitting with your team, figuring out what your content is going to look like for the next 30 days. Below are 20 things you can include that people will not only read but share.

1. **The Trends Manifesto.** You'll find this happening in the blogosphere starting in October and running through January. It'll either be the trends you are expecting to hit your industry in the next year or the three words people will use to drive their success. Both do extremely well. The trends manifesto provides you with an opportunity to shine as a leader in your industry. People want someone to look into a crystal ball and predict some of the things they should be watching for throughout the year. The three words, on the other hand, give people a sneak peak into you as a person and as a leader.

2. **The Pop Culture Tie-In.** Lots of really successful content creators take something that is happening with *The Kardashians*, or *Dancing with the Stars*, or the latest reality show and provide lessons related to their field.

3. **The Debate.** We often disagree with other voices on the Web, but we don't feel "safe" to voice our differing opinions. That's why you often hear things such as "echo chamber" and "yes men" when bloggers are discussed. Paul Sutton, a communications professional in the United Kingdom, creates the opportunity for debate a couple of times each year. He takes one side of an issue, and another blogger takes the other. They debate it and create a poll to let readers decide who wins. Giving people an opportunity to see two sides of something works incredibly well.

4. **The Good.** Remember how we talked about how sex sells earlier in the book? While people love good train wrecks, we also want to know how companies in our industry are doing things well. Interview organizations in your industry and highlight the good things they're doing through your content.

5. **The Bad.** It's no surprise the bad case studies are shared over and over and over again. When Chick-fil-A had their train wreck of an issue because their CEO came out against the gay and lesbian community, the best content was about why politics and religion in business are a bad idea and not about how the author felt personally about the company's leadership or the issues being dissected.

6. **The Ugly.** We already know people like train wrecks. They can't stop watching. If you can figure out how to write about one without attacking a person, it's going to be pretty popular. Ragan does a nice job of this quite often by using terms such as "most hated" in a headline. It grabs attention and makes people want to read *and* share.

7. **The Lists.** People love lists. We have so much information coming at us these days, and lists make it easier to scan and read quickly. If you integrate lists into your content, you'll find it's easily some of the most shared on your site. Test it out. No matter how you feel about it "cheapening" the reading experience, it works.

8. **Freebies.** Give stuff away! It might be a book a friend has written, a collection of free e-books available from other bloggers, or your own e-book. Doing this helps you begin to qualify prospects.

9. **Ranked Lists.** The organization Run, Walk, Ride puts together a list of the charities that raise the most money every year. They highlight the ones you'd expect, but also show how well some of the up-and-comers are doing. In 2013, they added an easily shared infographic for bloggers and journalists. It's a total win for them because they're highlighting their peers (and competitors) and driving significant top-of-the-funnel traffic to their site.

10. **Something of the Year.** Just like *People* produces its "sexiest man alive" issue, you can do the same for your niche. It may be an app of the month or a productivity tool. We do a live chat with an author on the third Wednesday of every month. There are lots of ideas for something of the week, month, or year.

11. **Book Reviews.** A Spin Sucks community member, Bhaskar Sarma,[3] suggests doing book reviews. He says, "Posts based around a book can be full of win. If that book is a must read in your industry, doing something as simple as summing up the key points or at least doing a review can easily give you 500–700 words. And, if you can tie in the lessons of the book with real world examples, then that's frosting on top of the cake."

12. **The Rant.** A rant can get people riled up about something and give them something to rally behind. That said, it's not something you should do a lot. Perhaps once a quarter is the right amount.

13. **Interviews.** Oprah, Katie Couric, Brian Williams, *Masterpiece Theater* know it: Interviews work well because you're giving people access to someone they wouldn't otherwise meet. It may be the big keynote speaker at your industry's annual conference, or someone you respect or admire for the movement they're making. This works with audio, video, and written text. Publish them in one spot on your blog or website so they're easy to find.

14. **Question of the Week.** Let people ask you a question they don't know the answer to, can't find on the Web, or are simply too lazy to do the research on their own. Incorporate your social networks, your blog, and your website in the answer.

15. **Education.** Go back into your education and previous experience archives. When the Internet and social media didn't exist, we had to rely solely on our education and experience. Now you can make comparisons as to how businesses used to roll versus how they roll today. Show your audience the similarities, or differences, and suggest strategies to capitalize on them.

16. **The Parable.** Tell a story to make a point in a post. It may be a difficult but incredibly interesting post to write. *The Paris Review* does a great job with this when they interview authors. It only comes out quarterly so it's worth your time investment to subscribe and read. Their writers will teach you how to tell a parable in a business setting.

17. **The Latest Trends.** Don't forget about the latest trends. While they may seem overdone, your audience is unique. They may not have seen what's happening in your industry and count on you to tell them.

18. **The Sales Questions.** Sit down with your sales team (or just yourself if you're the rainmaker) and ask what kinds of questions come up in meetings with prospects. That may include pricing, delivery, referrals, and point-of-differentiation. If you haven't already created content for these things, do it. Do it now! As you dig into this question, you'll hear deeper issues people want to know about before they buy. Create content around these things because, I guarantee, if something is coming up in sales meetings people are searching for it too. Be found for those questions.

---

3. https://twitter.com/#!/bhas

19. **Roundup of Voices.** There are some bloggers who do this very well. They'll ask the same question of five industry experts and create content around their answers. For Valentine's Day one year, HubSpot asked experts why businesses should create marketing that people love and want to share. They created a short e-book that included the quotes and fun images and let people download it for free. Lots of really great content without a ton of work on their part.

20. **The Smarty Pants.** Ike Pigott, a spokesman for Alabama Power, wrote "Eleven Words Guaranteed to Generate Killer Search Engine Traffic and Clicks." When you go to the page, all you find are those 11 words. His point? People are dying for the big secret on how to game the system. It's a get-rich-quick scheme, and it works for Ike in this instance because the other content he offers is extremely intelligent and very valuable. You can't get away with this a lot, but adding in some humor to prove a point can work occasionally.

The News Release

We've spent a lot of time talking about content—what works, what doesn't, what works in the short term, and what takes longer. This conversation won't end, even after you finish reading this book. Content includes blogging, white papers, podcasts, videos, e-books, in-depth articles, webinars, and more. It also includes news releases, which people claim dead at least once a month.

For the past several years, PR professionals have taken an interesting tack with their news releases. They write them, include links to the organization's website, and distribute on the wires. In the past, the search engines would see the links to the organization's website on all of the media sites and promote that site in the search results.

Let's say you write a news release about a new product you're launching. It's going to change the world and you're very excited about it. Your internal PR team or your external agency writes a news release that will accompany their personal phone calls and emails to journalists, but they also suggest you distribute the release on the newswire (PR Web, PR Newswire, or BusinessWire). That sounds great because it will not only gain you mentions on the world's biggest news sites, such as Bloomberg, Yahoo!, and the *Wall Street Journal*, it will provide that all-important high-authority link.

But Matt Cutts, a Google employee, recently wrote on his blog, "Links from your news releases don't have SEO value." He was ahead of the actual announcement. In August 2013, Google announced that using links in news releases[4] to increase your search engine results violates its Webmaster Guidelines and it'll begin to penalize the sites that practice this method. This means any news release that has keywords listed more than once, keywords included as anchor text, or links not marked as "nofollow" are penalized.

The following are the do's and don'ts of news release writing for the Web.

---

4. https://support.google.com/webmasters/answer/66356?hl=en

1. **Don't do keyword stuffing.** An old SEO trick, keyword stuffing, meant filling a web page with the same words or phrases over and over again so the search engines would look at that page as an "authority" on the topic. It might look like the following, with the keywords in italics: "Many organizations offer *wellness programs* to help employees reduce health-care costs. When employees participate in *wellness programs*, including exercise and healthy nutrition, the *wellness programs* offered from insurance companies are less expensive. If you want a healthy team, consider a *wellness program*."

   During the past several years, Google has penalized websites that practice this. Now it's going to do the same for the news releases you distribute online.

2. **Don't include duplicate content.** Most news releases are distributed on the wire, which multiple organizations grab content from. That means it's possible to have the same release—with the exact same copy—posted in multiple locations across the Web, including on your own website and many news websites. This is now against the rules. What that means for organizations such as BusinessWire and PR Newswire is they will likely create "nofollow" links in your releases and link to an original article so the search engines don't consider it duplicate content.

3. **Don't include standard links.** When you create web copy, the general rule is you want to have one external link for every 100 words. This rule still stands for web copy, but not for news releases. If your release has lots of links and follows that rule, your site can be penalized. It's best to create press releases with "nofollow" links so the search engines don't view them as gaming the system.

4. **Do include "nofollow" links.** A "nofollow" tag is something you add in the HTML code when you create a link in your release. It tells the search engines not to follow the link to your site, but the journalists who receive the release can still use it to get more information about your organization and its products or services. Simply add `rel="nofollow"` at the end of the hyperlink tag. For example, `<a href="http://www.spinsucks.com/" title="Spin Sucks" rel="nofollow">Visit Spin Sucks</a>`.

In today's fast paced digital world, it makes perfect sense for PRSA to constantly tweak the definition of what it is that we do. Technology is changing the way we communicate almost daily. A big, new social network pops up at least once a year. Google changes its algorithms monthly. Your website and blog have new competitors every day. Even if you're a thought leader in your industry because you do a great job with owned media, you will soon have new competitors you've never considered before.

It's impossible to keep up with everything. The very best thing you can do is continue to create valuable and interesting owned media, integrate it with the more traditional paid and earned media, and know as much as you can about how the search engines work to help people find you.

II

Scammers, Liars, and Beggars

4

Whisper Campaigns and Anonymous Attackers

In early 2009, the *Halifax-Plympton Reporter* received a letter to the editor urging people to "contact their Congressman about the Medicare Advantage program, a sort of privatized health plan paid for through the recipient's Medicare. There may be some interest in doing away with the program."

Seems benign enough, right? The letter was signed by a local resident, but it didn't mention the local Congressman, which the paper's editor found strange. So he called the man who wrote the letter and was astounded to learn the letter's "author" had no idea what he was talking about.

The editor filed the letter and went on about his day. About a week later, he received a phone call from a man who said he was calling on behalf of the person who wrote the letter. The editor told the caller what he had done and asked who he was and who he worked for. The caller declined to tell the editor who he was and hung up the phone. But what he didn't count on was caller ID. The editor traced it back to a high-powered lobbying and public affairs firm in D.C. It became pretty evident the firm was working for an organization with an interest in keeping Medicare Advantage in business.

The firm's site promises "grassroots communication," but this is downright astroturfing.

According to *Campaigns & Elections*, astroturfing is "a grassroots program that involves the instant manufacturing of public support for a point-of-view in which either uninformed activists are recruited or means of deception are used to recruit them."

At one time found only in politics, this practice has spread to the communications industry.

Genuine grassroots campaigns tend to have many people involved, but don't always have the money needed to support them. Think about Occupy Wall Street, or President Obama's 2008 bid for the White House, or campaigns designed to get television programs back on the air. They use the Web and social media to help further their ideals, but don't always have a lot of money behind them.

Astroturfing, though, tends to be flush with cash but people-poor...so the designers make up people. On the Web, they'll create fake personas or robots to spread the word. Offline, sophisticated computer databases, telephone banks, as well as hired organizers, are used to recruit and inspire less-informed activists to send letters to their elected officials or to the city's main newspaper. Ultimately, it ends up looking like there are many people up in arms about pending changes.

According to Wikipedia, these techniques have been used to

- Defeat President Clinton's proposed health care reform through a front group called Rx Partners, which was created by a public relations firm and the Coalition for Health Insurance Choices

- Oppose restrictions on smoking in public places through a front group called National Smokers Alliance, which was created by a global public relations firm

- Encourage people to buy Coke

- Generate news clips to assist Microsoft lobbyists in persuading U.S. state attorney generals not to join a class action suit against the company

While shocking, the good news is, as consumers, we're far more educated through information found on the Web, these kinds of campaigns are found very quickly, brought to the attention of influential journalists, and taken down.

"For years, Mark Zuckerberg, the chief executive of Facebook, has extolled the virtue of transparency, and he built Facebook accordingly. The social network requires people to use their real identity in large part because Mr. Zuckerberg says he believes that people behave better—and society will be better—if they cannot cloak their words or actions in anonymity," wrote the *New York Times* on May 13, 2011.

Enter a global public relations firm. They were hired to create a "whisper campaign" about Social Circle—an optional feature of Google that uses publicly available information from social networks to personalize search results.

The story goes like this: Two very high-profile former reporters-turned-PR-pros worked with journalists and bloggers to begin digging into Social Circle and writing negative stories about it. When pushed to reveal their client, they refused, and a blogger published their email exchange.

The initial email from the high-profile PR pro began, "I wanted to gauge your interest in authoring an op-ed this week for a top-tier media outlet on an important issue that I know you're following closely." He went on to describe the sweeping violations of user privacy at Google and how the blogger could use the information in his email to write the op-ed.

The blogger responded with, "Who is paying for this? (Not paying me, but paying you)."

The PR pro wrote, "Thanks for the prompt reply. I'm afraid I can't disclose my client yet. But all the information included in this email is publicly available. Any interest in pursuing this?"

The blogger, smart to these kinds of practices, denied the request and made the entire conversation public, which made national news and required the Public Relations Society of America (PRSA) to get involved, from an ethics point-of-view.

This is common practice in Silicon Valley. PR professionals are hired to help create negative stories about one's competition.

It happens in Hollywood, too. During the 2013 Oscars season, you might remember seeing stories such as, "Can you believe *Zero Dark Thirty*? The Academy is never going to vote for a movie that justifies torture." Or "If you want historical accuracy, don't watch *Argo*. The suspense when they're leaving the airport? That never happened." Or "Come on, *Lincoln*! Mary Todd Lincoln never attended debates, but there she is in the visitor's galley in the movie."

These comments typically begin with publicists or "Oscar-campaign consultants" who have off-the-record chats with reporters and voters. They don't talk about the great attributes of the movies, actors, or directors they represent; rather, they point out the flaws in their competitors. And some of these stories are created by the media looking to increase eyeballs and win in the ratings wars.

The Academy has tried to discourage the negativity by imposing a one-year suspension of membership for first-time violators, but this rule is hardly ever enforced because most whisper campaigners are too smart to malign their competition publicly. They never put anything in writing, including in email.

The idea of whisper campaigns began, not surprisingly, during wartime, because it is an effective and inexpensive way to create protests, support stand-offs, and exercise national will without using the military. From there, it has seeped into politics, the tobacco industry, Hollywood, and now Silicon Valley.

But it isn't limited to those few instances. In business, companies hire employees to create fake social media accounts to post comments on blogs, forums, chat rooms, and social networks. They try to steer conversations in a desired direction or post negative responses that rile up the community.

For instance, a defense contractor that works with the government was found to be mounting an attack against WikiLeaks when they were hacked by Anonymous (the hackers responsible for a lot of the tightly secured information that throughout the years has been leaked to WikiLeaks).

In the documents they found and leaked, there was information about how to create personas to attack journalists, bloggers, and commenters to "smear enemies and distort the truth."

Here's a quote from the leaked materials: "To build this capability we will create a set of personas on twitter, blogs, forums, buzz, and myspace under created names that fit the profile (satellitejockey, hack3rman, etc.). These accounts are maintained and updated automatically through RSS feeds, retweets, and linking together social media commenting between platforms. With a pool of these accounts to choose from, once you have a real name persona you create a Facebook and LinkedIn account using the given name, lock those accounts down and link these accounts to a selected # of previously created social media accounts, automatically pre-aging the real accounts."

Another document describes how they use automation so one persona can represent many different people with the stroke of a key. "Using the assigned social media accounts we can automate the posting of content that is relevant to the persona. In this case there are specific social media strategy website RSS feeds we can subscribe to and then repost content on twitter with the appropriate hashtags. In fact using hashtags and gaming some location based check-in services we can make it appear as if a persona was actually at a conference and introduce [sic] himself/herself to key individuals as part of the exercise, as one example. There are a variety of social media tricks we can use to add a level of realness to all fictitious personas."

That's just another example of how gigantic organizations are gaming the system, lying and stealing, and developing groups of "people" to provide opinions about an issue.

In the past, these things worked fairly well. It was difficult to not only prove it was happening, but to get the attention of journalists to tell the story. But there's a new sheriff in town, named social media. Because of him, everyone has a megaphone. When you are found out, people are all too happy to rip you down from the fake proverbial pedestal.

Brian Solis, principal analyst at Altimeter Group, a prominent blogger, keynote speaker, and author of several books, did a test to promote the launch of "The End of Business as Usual." Using a service called Let Me Tweet That For You, he created a bunch of tweets from celebrities such as Donald Trump and Ellen DeGeneres that are made to look like they endorse his book (Figure 4.1).

Of course, the tweets Brian created aren't real and he never actually sent them. He created them only to show it's important to confirm any information we see online that seems strange, because it most likely is. A great example of this is the photos of Abraham Lincoln you see floating around the Web that display quotes, supposedly by him, on how to behave online. Of course, Lincoln didn't say those things, but people continue to share the quotes. After all, if it's on the Internet; it must be true.

Figure 4.1 *Let Me Tweet That For You allows you to create fake tweets from real people.*

After Brian opened the kimono, so to speak, and showed what he did and why he did it, we took to the Web to create a fake tweet from a colleague, saying she loves working with me (Figure 4.2).

Figure 4.2 *A test to create a fake tweet about myself from a friend and colleague.*

Admittedly, it's kind of fun to create tweets saying awesome things about yourself that look like they're coming from your friends or colleagues. And the good news is the service doesn't allow you to actually tweet what you've created. Instead, it generates a tweet that says, "Check out what @belllindsay just said **http://lemmetweetthatfor-you.com/t/2tl99k** Site by @okfocus."

So Lindsay would be alerted if I tweeted that, and anyone following would be directed to the site where it was generated. No harm, no foul, right?

Not so fast. What if trust has now completely eroded? People are astroturfing and creating whisper campaigns and writing fake reviews—and now, faking tweets. What next?

As it turns out, there are lots of blog posts, forums, and how-to sites written for people who want to start their own whisper campaigns. If you'd like to go that route, stop reading and donate this book to a library. You're not going to learn how to do that here.

Trolls and Anonymous Attackers

There are quite a few things you can do to dissuade anonymous attackers. Use Livefyre as your commenting system, which forces commenters to have an account (usually with one of the social networks); build a strong community of people who can quickly recognize those who are there only to cause trouble; and have guidelines that clearly state comments will be deleted if you swear, make up facts, or are intent on damaging someone's reputation (or that of someone in the community) through libel. Ninety-nine point nine nine percent of the time, people are very professional, fun, and kind to one another.

But there will be that one time when you are attacked personally, and anonymously.

When you discover negative comments, you can quickly do some research to find out who the people are. Track their accounts back through Livefyre, and after a few clicks, you'll discover whether it's a real person or not. Sometimes you'll find there is a content farm in another part of the world that is set on creating negative comments to engage authors in conversation, eventually gaming the Google rating system.

Rather than engage those "people," delete the comments and ban the users from commenting on your site. It does take some time, but it's well worth it. Don't be rushed. Take that time. Because if you don't, the attackers win. Situations like this make the online world a bit scary. People will say negative things about you. They will criticize you. When this happens, take out the emotion, listen to what people have to say, admit when you're wrong, and say you're sorry.

Except when the attackers are anonymous. The culture of the Web allows for anonymous attackers known as "trolls": the people who say, from behind a computer screen, things they would never say in public. We see this with online bullying of children and teenagers, and we see it, via adults for the most part, in business. The Web provides a "safe" world where trolls can wield power and influence others. Unlike most real-world bullies, though, anonymous attackers can find a large ready-made audience to consistently engage, vote up their content, share it, and provide serious ego-stroking without negative consequences. In fact, some sites offer real-world bonus items for popular content—no matter if it's harmful or not. But, like real-world bullies, trolls need to get a rise out of their victims to enjoy the interaction. When you don't "feed the trolls," you disgrace them and make them feel irrelevant.

It really isn't unlike serial killers or mass murderers (particularly in the United States) who kill for the publicity and fame they know they'll achieve. Those 15 minutes of fame come at any price…but they're willing to do what it takes to get them. The same thing happens online (even if not at the expense of people's lives) and trolls will do what they can simply to get a rise out of you.

Reddit is a site that allows anyone to register with any username. You can submit and vote on content, all anonymously. You're also able to start a forum dedicated to your hobbies or interests, known as a subreddit. During the Boston Marathon bombings, there was an entire subreddit dedicated to the manhunt—which gave you more accurate and timely information than the news. In fact, reading that stream—which was hooked into the Boston police scanner—revealed to the online world that the second suspect had been caught a full five minutes before the news reported it.

During the 2012 Presidential campaign, President Obama became the first sitting president to participate in a Reddit AMA (Ask Me Anything) feature. People from all around the world participated, and he answered questions about space exploration, Internet freedom, his favorite basketball player (Michael Jordan), and work-life balance. The hour-long Q&A session gave Reddit mass legitimacy and let the site open itself up not only to the typical web geeks, but also to mainstream news and political junkies.

But the site isn't all for the greater good. Because Reddit allows anonymity and the policy itself is very lenient on offensive speech, it has bred an underground of trolls, attackers, and downright bad people.

In October of 2012, a man known as Violentacrez—one of the biggest trolls on Reddit—was found out by *Gawker*. You see, he'd been posting images of scantily-clad underage girls on the Internet, which is what began the deeper investigation into who he really was. But more than that, if you found images of racism, porn, incest, or other highly offensive things on Reddit, it was almost certain Violentacrez was behind them. In fact, he created a subreddit called "Creepshots" where users posted covert photos taken of women in public—usually close-ups of their body parts. And the subreddit thrived.

Violentacrez created another subreddit called Jailbait, with the sole purpose of "creating a safe place for people sexually attracted to underage girls to share their photo stashes." While you or I might call those people pedophiles, the subreddit called them "ephebophiles." Violentacrez and his fellow moderators worked hard to make sure every girl posted in Jailbait was underage. They deleted any photos whose subjects looked like they were older than 16. It soon became one of the most popular subreddits on the site and the term "jailbait" was the second biggest search term for the site. Eventually it landed on CNN, and Anderson Cooper called out both Reddit and Violentacrez. The subreddit was banned—reluctantly because it's against the Reddit terms of service to police the user content and because their community was incensed at the very idea of being "policed"—and, with it, all content featuring minors.

Lock up your children! Protect the women! Throw away the keys!

Like "real life" bullies, trolls need to get a rise out of their victims if they are to enjoy the interaction. But it's not all as bad as Violentacrez, particularly in the business world. Yes, you will have trolls attacking you, especially as you participate more and grow your brand online. Yes, they will make you angry and emotional. Yes, they will get a rise out of you. But it's how you handle them that makes all the difference between them feeling like a mosquito bite in the middle of summer, or them forcing your focus away from your job completely.

The best way to stop trolls is to create an environment that is unfriendly to trolling. We've done that on Spin Sucks by carefully cultivating a professional, kind, and smart community. We painstakingly review all comments and determine their validity. If we remove someone, we explain to everyone else why we did that, citing something in our policy the person violated. Today, the community does the rest of the work. The good news is it's unlikely you'll be trolled—unless you're Coke or GE or Facebook—until you've built a name for your organization online. With that, hopefully, comes a community of people who adore you—or at least respect you. They'll stick up for you, often without you having to ask.

Public Attackers

More likely, however, you will find you know your attackers. It could be your colleagues, a former employee, a disgruntled customer, a competitor, or a blogger who doesn't see eye-to-eye with your business practices. Trolls can be right inside your organization, using their keyboards to harass their colleagues.

A few years ago, morale dropped considerably inside our organization. We couldn't figure out what was going on. People were nice to one another in our weekly staff meetings. They joked and laughed with one another. Nothing seemed amiss when you saw the team interacting. But get someone alone, and all they did was complain about how much they hated their job or their colleagues or the work they were doing. People kept calling in sick. Some who were always on time—or early—began coming in late and leaving early. Anonymous employee satisfaction surveys showed a huge drop from the previous quarter, but we couldn't get to the bottom of it. Until an email was sent not meant for the eyes of the CEO.

As it turns out, the mid-level managers were bullying the young professionals through email. And it was horrible. Some of the things they were saying to one another would make even the most hardened person blush. It was not only unprofessional, it was mean, rude, and disturbing. It was astonishing and it was tearing down our culture. It became pretty apparent two things were happening: First, there was a ringleader (who we discovered later), and second, they were saying things to one another in email they *never* would say in person. But here's the catch: In the office, they sat less than 20 feet away from one another. So, to their faces (and to the executive team), they were all smiles and jokes and fun. But behind the computer screen? Well, it was appalling.

So, we banned email. Not external email—of course they still had to be able to email clients. But they were not allowed to email one another. They had to—gasp!—talk to one another. Actually stand up and peer over the cubicle walls to have a conversation, or walk around a wall and through a door to talk to someone else. Not only did it work like a charm, with morale rising almost visibly; the ringleader was found out and promptly fired.

This is a case of how troll-like behavior can happen in person and likely something most business leaders have encountered at some point in their career. As you begin to think about how to manage this kind of behavior online, remember there are tips and tricks you learned in your climb to the top that will help. The behavior is different, the tips aren't different, just the tools are different.

Keeping that in mind, trolls can also be bloggers who—though they don't work with you and never have—have an opinion on how you run your business and aren't afraid to tell the world how they feel about it, using search-optimized posts to make sure their message stays on the first page of Google results forever.

Case in point. There is an entrepreneur in Los Angeles who is trying to change for the better how premature babies receive nutrition in a neonatal intensive care unit. Premature babies are more prone to diseases and bacteria as their little bodies grow outside of the womb. One of the worst diseases—necrotizing enterocolitis (or NEC)—kills nearly 80 percent of premature babies who develop it. The risk of a baby developing it can be greatly reduced if fed a 100 percent human milk diet. Because mom's milk won't have fully come in when a baby arrives early, she needs help supplementing with a fortifier. In the past, most hospitals would supplement with cow's milk to provide the extra fat and calories a baby needs to grow and thrive.

When the American Academy of Pediatrics made a recommendation that babies younger than six months old be fed a 100 percent human milk diet, a nonprofit model popped up to take donated breast milk and provide it to hospitals for the NICU.

This entrepreneur, who has experience in the blood industry, wanted to see breast milk tested at the same level as other bodily fluids. Therefore, he took the reigns of a for-profit company to put the donated milk through a battery of tests to make sure it was safe, then develop a fortifier, and get it into the hospitals to help save lives.

But, as a for-profit organization, they see a lot of negative blog posts written about them and their business model, some even going as far as to attack this man and his executive team personally by calling them "evil" and "blood suckers."

We have worked with hundreds of clients throughout the years, so we have seen unethical, dishonest, and flat out wrong business practices. This entrepreneur and his team are not any of those things. Their vision is to help the world's tiniest, most precious babies. The babies who are born weighing less than three pounds. The babies who can't nurse. The babies who can take only drops of milk at a time. The babies so underdeveloped they have a fairly high risk of contracting an intestinal disease—which is almost always a death sentence.

They have spent years—and millions of dollars—on research to make sure premature babies have the nutrition they need in their first few weeks on earth. They have created testing no one else does to ensure the safety of their product. And, yes, they are a for-profit company. It costs money to run all those tests. But there are some bloggers who have a big problem with the for-profit angle and have taken it upon themselves to tell the world how this big, bad, for-profit company is taking advantage of parents who have premature babies.

These bloggers who fight them with their words refuse to meet with anyone from the company, and refuse to take a tour of the facilities. They just sit behind their computer screens and throw bombs on the Web for moms to find when they're researching the best thing to do for their newly born premature baby.

The company became a client because we believe in their mission and vision. As we began work with them, we set a plan in place to not only respond to all of the criticism, but to invite the bloggers into the California headquarters to tour the facility and meet the researchers and scientists behind the product. Most, of course, declined, citing busy lives or not being able to take time off work, but a few have taken us up on the offer...and almost all of them changed their minds about this big, bad, evil empire.

For those who declined, however, the conversation was very public in the comments of each blog post. Some parents commented saying they appreciate that the company responds and is open to the criticism. Other parents have said they're creeped out when the organization comments on their posts. But something magical began to happen: Parents chimed in saying things such as, "If you use the company name in your updates, you should expect they're paying attention" or "I imagine the company has Google Alerts or some kind of monitoring set up so they know when they're mentioned online." A community not intentionally built is now sticking up for the company, and it's a great thing.

Typically people who post under their own names just want to be heard. We all want to know someone is listening and will help us with our issues or concerns. A simple "We hear what you're saying. If you wouldn't mind sending us your email address or phone number, we're happy to talk to you about this" works 99.9 percent of the time. Think about the last time you were unhappy with a product or service. Did you have to go through the phone tree that never got you anywhere? Have you posted something online to never hear from the organization? It's super frustrating, right?

When I speak, I tell this story quite often. I tell it so often, in fact, I've heard rumors that other speakers tell it, too.

In 2008, I was flying to Denver to speak to two CEO groups for Vistage International. It was the week before the Memorial Day weekend, and we'd planned to meet our friends, after my work was complete, in Beaver Creek for the long weekend. I had rented a car for Wednesday through the following Monday.

I "grew up" in a big PR firm where the car rental company of choice was Avis. Because I've traveled at least once a week for most of my career, I was part of their Princess Platinum club (I made that up—it was whichever club is their highest). That status traveled with me after I left the PR firm and started my own business, and I kept it because I continued that kind of travel schedule. I had no reason to leave them and I was treated very well.

The Vistage speaking coordinator called to see if I could add a day on the front end of the trip to speak to one more group. Not a problem on my end, and we called Avis to have them add to the reservation. We were told they were out of cars and I'd have to find one for that first day somewhere else. Politely explaining I was in their Princess Platinum, we asked if they could send a car from another location. The customer service rep said they had a car at another location, but that I would have to "take a cab" to get there.

At this point, it was very early in the world of Twitter, but being an avid user (especially back then), I went online to see if they had an account there. Guess what? They did! Their Twitter handle is (or was at the time) @wetryharder. So I tweeted, "@wetryharder Having a problem extending an existing reservation in Denver. Can you help?"

Crickets. Nothing. Not a peep. But a few minutes later, Hertz tweeted me. They said, "So sorry to hear about our competition. We can help!" They helped me get a car for my entire trip, gave me the same status I had at Avis, and sent me on my merry way.

About a week after I got home, Hertz tweeted me and asked how the trip was, how the car was, if customer service was helpful—they were gathering market research. Then they said if I rented from them again, they would give me their Gold status for free. I did and I haven't gone back to Avis since then.

Remember this was in May of 2008. In September of that same year, I received a letter in the mail from Avis asking what it would take to get my business back. Four months had gone by before they realized someone who typically rented at least one car a week from them was gone. The original tweet went unanswered. Hertz was monitoring the social networks and Avis was not. And they lost a loyal customer because of it.

Sometimes we just want to be heard.

The Trolls, Critics, and Attackers

Livefyre is a plugin you can use in WordPress that allows people to comment on your blog. It's one of the best because it cuts down on not just spam, but anonymous attackers. It requires people to create an account, which automatically dissuades most from commenting anonymously. But there are a few who will create fake accounts for the sheer purpose of attacking you or your community. You can't prevent people from saying negative things on your social network pages, but—for the most part—those are real people, too.

If there are negative comments, remember most people want to be heard. First, get to the bottom of the complaint. Sometimes what you perceive as someone being a troll or stirring up dirt for the sake of doing so will turn out to be a valid complaint. Figure out where the complaint is coming from and whether or not they're right. While you're doing research and talking with your team, respond immediately to the person with, "We hear you and we're getting to the bottom of this. Give us a few hours and we'll update you along the way."

Then do as you said you would. If the complaint is valid, comment again and ask the person to privately send you their contact information. Take the conversation offline and help them with the issue.

A company of 70 assisted-living and retirement homes in the Midwest hired us a few years ago to see if social media could help them communicate with the children of their residents. Knowing, of course, the children are typically the decision makers.

Through our research, we discovered a Wii had been installed in every common living area throughout the entire organization…and residents were playing games on the consoles. Such a fun little nugget—we filed that away for later use, hoping we could eventually use it. When tasked with the idea of using social media to engage the resident's children, we knew we had to find a way to showcase these Wii competitions and see if we could extend them beyond each community.

Coming up on March Madness, we suggested they create the NCAA of Wii players and have the residents compete with one another. As they played, it was recorded in real time and uploaded to the community's website and through Facebook. Then friends, families, and other residents could vote on the winner for each specific community. Just like in college basketball, each team could advance on and eventually face off in a "national" championship. It was a lot of fun, and people really got into it—sharing the videos, asking for votes, and suggesting games to play. And, let's be real, retired people playing Wii is pretty fantastic.

One week, in the middle of all of this, the CEO and I were traveling to a conference together. The night before it began, we were in the hotel bar chatting about work and he asked to see this creation of ours. I pulled out my laptop, opened Facebook, and scrolled through the different pages to show him how active and engaged his communities were in this contest.

And then something alarming happened. As we were scrolling through, someone posted on the page a very scathing comment. It was unprofessional, it was mean, and it used a lot of swear words. The woman was the daughter of a resident, and she was angry after receiving a call from her mother, who was extremely upset about her visit to the resident's beautician that day. Apparently she'd had her hair colored and it turned blue. Not an uncommon issue among elderly women, but blue hair is very upsetting.

The CEO backed away from the computer and put his hands up as if it were on fire. We talked about what to do, and then he timidly put his hands on the keyboard and typed, "I'm the CEO and I just saw this. Would you mind sending me your phone number so I can call you?"

The woman did so and he took out his cell phone and called her. Right then and there. He learned this wasn't the first time her mother's hair had been turned blue by the hairdresser and the salon refused to do anything about it. She was upset at their lack of empathy and customer service. He let her vent for a good 10 minutes and then offered her mom three free salon visits. He also called the salon manager and had a talk with her to be sure that never happened again.

The woman was so pleased with the responsiveness, she went back to the Facebook page and posted about it. Today she is one of the company's biggest fans.

Of course, it's not always going to be the most senior person in the organization to respond to a fan's criticism, but it isn't hard to turn a critic into a fan if you apologize and fix the situation.

When this happens to you—and it will happen to you—there is a four-step process you should employ.

1. **Get to the bottom of the initial complaint.** Sometimes the critics might be right. If they are right and not complaining just to complain, listening to what they have to say will lead to identifying and solving an issue before it grows too large or gets out of hand.

2. **Consider the source.** On the other hand, if the person is there only to cause trouble, you can ignore them. Responding will only add fuel to the fire, which is what these people feed on. Most of you will know who your trolls are because they show up consistently and try to take you down. All of our clients have a list of people they should ignore. Consider it your mental black list.

3. **Weigh the influence of the person.** If the critic isn't on your black list and you're not sure of their complaint, consider how much influence they have within your industry. While you don't want to be disrespectful of anyone complaining, you can definitely prioritize responses based on the person's influence.

4. **Reply and then listen.** If the complaint is valid, you should reply to the person—publicly—and then ask them to provide their contact information through a private message. Replying publicly allows other people to see you're handling the situation, and then you can take the conversation offline. In the very best case, the person will post publicly again after the situation is solved, as happened with my friend.

Seven Steps to Dealing with Criticism

All of this isn't meant to scare you. Most of you will have sites, communities, and content that increases your brand awareness, helps you position yourself in your market, and generates new leads. But there will be occasions when people will want to tear you down. Sometimes those people will be anonymous—in those cases, you can decide to ignore them. In other cases, they'll be people you already know—they may have vocally complained about you in the past, or they may be a friend turned foe.

Whoever it is, it's important to be strategic about dealing with criticism. The following seven steps will help.

1. **Create an internal policy.** Everyone on your team—both internally and externally—needs to understand what your policy is for managing criticism online. A bad situation can be made worse by a well-intentioned employee or external partner who doesn't understand your policy. The policy should lay out who will respond to critics online, what they'll say, how quickly they'll respond, and what to do if someone not authorized to comment sees or receives a comment.

2. **Be cautious.** When dealing with critics, particularly if they're anonymous, you don't know how severe the reaction could be or how successful they may be in creating an online crisis involving hundreds or thousands of others. A good rule of thumb is to publicly say you hear them and you'd like to discuss offline. Then take it to the phone or in person. Get it out of writing so you can hear the tone of voice and see body language. The last thing you want to do is get defensive or engage in a back-and-forth debate online.

3. **Assume the best.** Even if you think the answer is obvious or right in front of their face, sometimes the critic is misinformed, or doesn't know where to look for the information on your site, or may be unwilling to search. When they complain about the obvious things, be helpful, pleasant, and nondefensive. You should never assume malicious intent until you've covered the obvious.

4. **Consider the medium.** Unless you run a sports, religious, or news site, it's unlikely anonymous trolls will want to spend their every waking moment criticizing you. So keep your goals in mind. Consider the medium of the criticism. If it's directly on your blog or on Facebook, it's far more difficult to ignore than in a tweet.

5. **Deleting posts.** While deleting posts may remove the damage for the time being, when people discover you're doing so, they'll take you to task for that...and it won't be pretty. Consider a politician who lies about his affair. Soon enough we all find out; cue news conference, with (or without) his family standing next to him, to admit the affair he lied about for months. It's far worse to be found out later than to attempt to ignore it to begin with. And, when you're transparent about your blemishes, an amazing thing happens: Your community comes to your defense.

6. **Use common sense.** Take your corporate hat off and think like a human being. No one wants to be talked to in corporate jargon or be showered with pre-approved PR messages. Be understanding, listen, and make things right. Don't act like a robot that can only repeat one or two messages. Use common sense when responding. Ask yourself if it's a real complaint or someone just harassing you. If it's the former, be patient and give the person time to vent their frustrations.

7. **Have a written external policy.** The policy should describe when you will delete comments or ban a commenter, and establishes the tone of the conversation allowed on the site. For instance, the policy at Spin Sucks is that you can't swear (we'll edit out the swear words if you do) and the discourse must be professional. We once had a troll who copied and pasted his rude comment to the top of the

stream every time the community pushed it down. He had been responded to, so we told him that if he continued to do that, his comments would be deleted and he would be banned. He stopped doing it. The written policy helps you moderate the conversation in a professional but open way.

It's a very uncomfortable position to be in. None of us want to be criticized. But, as the saying goes, if people either love you or hate you, you're doing something right.

5

Media Manipulation

In September 2013, the *New York Times* ran an editorial penned by President Vladimir Putin.[1] In it, published on the anniversary of 9/11 and just one day after President Obama spoke to the country about Syria, Putin decries the United Nations as coming close to suffering the same fate as the League of Nations, which collapsed because it lacked real leverage. He went on to say that the potential strike against Syria by the United States, opposed by many countries, could result in more innocent lives lost.

Politics aside, the editorial created quite a stir in the PR industry. Ketchum, a well-respected global agency, works with the Russian government; they were the ones to work with the *Times* in placing the editorial in the opinion pages.

Working with foreign governments is not a bad thing. In fact, it helps promote peace and assists in the ability for countries to work together. Placing editorials for business, political, or religious leaders is not a bad thing. In fact, an American newspaper printing words from a foreign country leader is not a bad thing. But a nonprofit newsroom ProPublica is calling for increased transparency in dealings between media and PR professionals, stating that readers have a right to know how the editorial came to be in the newspaper to begin with.

It's a blurry line, for sure. Should there be a footnote at the end of every written piece saying which PR firms or professionals helped with the story? Should the evening news have it included in the ticker along the bottom of the screen? Should ESPN highlight every agent they worked with to get an interview with an athlete? Should

---

1. www.nytimes.com/2013/09/12/opinion/putin-plea-for-caution-from-russia-on-syria.html

every politician's press secretary be named when a story—good or bad—runs about their candidate?

One job of the public relations professional is working with journalists in the story development, creating interview opportunities, and making sure the organizations for which they work are highlighted in positive and meaningful ways. It's been this way for more than a hundred years. Nothing has changed. Or has it?

Enter Ryan Holiday, the author of *Trust Me, I'm Lying.* The premise of his book is how easy it is to manipulate the media for your own gain. The first half of his book provides case study after case study on how he created fake personas to con journalists into interviewing him as a reputable source. Using "Help a Reporter Out" (HARO), a free service that puts sources in touch with journalists, Holiday decided to respond to each and every query he saw, whether he knew anything about the topic or not. Nor did he do it alone. He enlisted an assistant to use his name to field as many requests as the two of them could humanly handle.

He expected it to take months of meticulous navigation, but within a few weeks, he found himself with more requests than he could handle. The interviews began to roll in. In a *Reuters* story, he talked about Generation Yikes, the group of young savers who are avoiding buying stocks. On ABC News, he talked about how long he's suffered from insomnia. At CBS, he told an embarrassing spell check story, and at MSNBC, he pretended someone sneezed on him while working at Burger King. At Manitouboats.com, he offered helpful tips for winterizing your boat. But the crème de la crème was when he was interviewed for a *New York Times* article about vinyl records.

As it turns out, he is an expert on none of these things. He does not suffer from insomnia nor collect vinyl records. He never sent an embarrassing email or worked at Burger King. He talked with journalists about these topics, under assumed names, and made up his tips, tricks, and stories. But the scary thing is that every media outlet ran his information without checking to see if what he said was true.

There are many stories about whisper campaigns, astroturfing, fake personas, and fake reviews. If there is a system, people will game it. No wonder ProPublica is calling for more transparency and better disclosure. We can be better. We have to be better. Great companies have great stories to tell. Hiring PR professionals to stir up controversy or whisper lies about your competitors isn't necessary. Making up personas or paying people to write reviews is unethical. Running an ethically sound company that gives back to its community *and* provides value to its shareholders is hard. It takes a long time to see results. The saying, "Nice guys always finish last," is true for that very reason. You may get quick results doing things the easy way, but they're never long lasting. Remember, this is a marathon, not a sprint.

To be a great company with great stories to tell, you have to act like a great company. In the October 2013 issue of *Harvard Business Review*,[2] the former executive vice

---

2. http://hbr.org/2013/10/dont-spin-a-better-story-be-a-better-company/ar/1

president of corporate affairs for Walmart, Leslie Dach, talks about how the giant low-price retailer began to evolve into a better company.

After Hurricane Katrina hit New Orleans, Walmart mobilized its employees to provide meals, emergency supplies, and cash. Two months later, then-CEO Lee Scott gave an internal speech in which he asked, "What would it take for Walmart to be at our best all the time? What if we used our size and resources to make this country, and this earth, an even better place for all of us? And what if we could do that and build a stronger business at the same time?"

After that speech, the company set its goals for sustainability, waste reduction, and the empowerment of women. Today, the goals of every employee include getting to that new vision. Because of these efforts, the company's story becomes easy to tell. They don't have to make things up, they don't have to lie about their competitors, and they don't have to place fake stories in the media.

In fact, they work to create new products that live up to the now famous company speech, which develops a halo effect that turns their critics into brand loyalists.

Take EDF, as an example. Michelle Harvey, a senior manager for retail at EDF, has lived in Bentonville, Ark., for the past several years to work with Walmart to find ways to bring healthier products to market. She and her team highlight the ingredients in products they believe need to be replaced.

Walmart is not only listening, they created a chemicals policy to bring better ingredients into its home and personal care products. They've truly set out to do the best thing, not just for their shareholders but for their customers, their communities, and the world.

Great companies don't lie. They don't steal. They don't cheat their employees. They don't become greedy. They don't allow people to behave badly just because that generates a lot of revenue. Great companies stop and listen to criticism. They commit to getting better, they set goals and a vision larger than themselves, and they truly behave better. When all of that happens, the storytelling is easy.

Build Relationships and Let the Rest Fall into Place

Let's say you have a great company. You behave ethically. You have great stories to tell. Your employees are active in your communities and do interesting things in their personal lives. Your customers are successful and have intriguing stories to tell. How do you go about letting the world know?

There is a lot of information online about how to do your own media relations. *Inc.* ran a story in July 2013, called "How to Do Your Own PR," in which sales guru Geoffrey James offered advice to business owners.[3]

---

3. www.inc.com/geoffrey-james/how-to-do-your-own-pr.html

He wrote, "I know people who are paying as much as $10,000 a month to a PR firm and getting very little out of it. And that's sad, because PR—getting positive media coverage—isn't all that difficult. Here's how it's done."

Geoffrey proposes an outline:

1. Devise a story worth writing about.
2. Create nuggets to insert into the story.
3. Offer yourself as a source.
4. Control the interview.

Never mind the fact PR is *not* about getting positive media coverage. Media relations, one tactic used in a PR program, is about getting positive media coverage. This advice makes it seem too simple. Yes, you have a great story to tell. Perhaps it's about sustainability, waste reduction, or the empowerment of women. Maybe you hire people with disabilities, people who have gone on to push the envelope with great personal accomplishments, such as climbing Mt. Hood unassisted. Or maybe you have customers who run successful businesses and use your product in new and interesting ways. Those are great nuggets you can insert into the story. You can even offer yourself as a source, which we'll talk about later in this chapter.

But you cannot control the interview. If a journalist feels like you're stalling on them or trying to control the agenda, they will eat you alive. Have you ever seen a politician interviewed on television who, when asked a question about something he or she doesn't want to answer, tries to force an agenda with a comment such as, "I can't talk about that, but what I can tell you about is my policy on healthcare"? Do you lose respect for the person when you hear that? Roll your eyes?

The same happens when you try to control your interview with a journalist. While you can't control your interviews, you should go into every one with a list of things you want to talk about, messages you want to relay, and well thought through answers to questions you will likely be asked.

With all the advice doled out every day on this topic on the Web, the important thing is to think about telling your story to the media in this way: You are building relationships with human beings. It's a give-and-take relationship. If you have journalists in your industry who focus on your niche, if there are business reporters you'd like to know, or if there are bloggers who could have an effect on your storytelling, start out by introducing yourself to them. Nurture that relationship. Give them something that doesn't do anything for you—for example, be a valuable industry resource. Eventually, you'll feel comfortable pitching a story to them, or they may even start asking how they can help you.

Building relationships takes time. It's a give-and-take. A marathon, not a sprint.

The article James wrote for *Inc.* starts out well. You do have to have a story. Having a new product, launching a new company, having a famous investor is not a story. To figure out what might be interesting to the journalists and bloggers you'll be pitching, you have to read what they're already writing.

It takes a lot of time and energy to do media relations really well. If you want to do it on your own (though it's sometimes far less expensive to hire a professional the first time around), here are some things to consider.

1. **Read blogs, publications, and online sites, watch the programs and listen to the shows where you want to appear.** It takes time, but it works because you figure out what the journalist, blogger, producer, or host really care about. Either your story fits or it doesn't. If it doesn't, no matter how badly you want a story in that publication, move on.

2. **Personalize your pitch.** Rosemary O'Neill, a co-founder of Social Strata, the makers of Hoop.la, decided to offer unlimited paid time off to her employees. The company has an office in Seattle, and Rosemary reads a *Seattle Times* journalist daily. She already knew what the journalist covers, and knew what would be interesting to her. She sent a two-sentence email about the new policy, and the journalist ran a story about it. But it didn't end there. National media picked it up as a new business trend, and Social Strata was put on the map as a trend-setting tech company.

3. **Comment on blog posts and articles.** This is the very best way for a journalist or blogger to get to know you. When you make smart comments on the articles they're producing, you build a relationship. Once you've built a relationship, they are much more willing to talk to you about your story. Some, in fact, will even help you mold the story if it's not an exact fit.

4. **Don't send a long email.** We are all busy. If you send an email that has everything anyone could ever possibly want to know about you, it won't be read. Take the approach Rosemary used and send a quick, attention grabbing email. The details can come later.

5. **Lose the idea of control.** Yes, when you give an interview, you should be prepared. You should ask the journalist or blogger ahead of time what kinds of questions you can expect to be asked. Use those questions to figure out what you want to say. But you cannot control the end result messaging. Your one or two messages might get repeated, but you cannot control how the conversation goes.

6. **Use the social networks.** If you have targeted publications or journalists in your industry, find them on their social networks. Find them on Twitter, then add them to a Twitter list so you see everything they tweet. Find a reason to connect with them there, even if it's just to introduce yourself, and keep the conversation going every day. Soon enough you'll find something they are working on that is a fit for you.

7. **Read their articles.** Unless they're on TV, most journalists have something you can read and comment on. Many will read the comments on their articles to

source new people to call. If you offer a differing opinion or provide more information on a topic, it's likely they will contact you for future stories.

8.   **Send something in the mail.** The joke among authors is, when you publish a book, you get an expensive business card. But it works really well as a gift to journalists whose radar you want to get on. If you haven't written a book, send a copy of a book from an author you admire. Even a handwritten note works extremely well in today's fast-paced, impersonal digital world.

9.   **Personalize your pitches.** It's pretty easy to write a news release about your latest big "new thing," copy it into an email, add a bunch of email addresses, and press Send. But that rarely works. You've spent all this time getting to know your industry journalists. Don't insult them by sending them the same thing you sent to everyone else on your list.

10.   **Be available to talk about industry trends.** There will be times you don't have any new news to share, or the news you do have won't fit what your targeted journalists are writing about. However, they may draw on you to comment on industry trends or news. Even if it may be just a quote in a bigger story, be helpful as often as possible. The "you scratch my back" thing comes into play, and you might end up with a bigger story centered on you.

Going through this takes time. You hire a professional not just because they have relationships you need. It's because—if they're good—they work on this every single day. But you *can* do it yourself if you're willing to roll up your sleeves, get your hands a little dirty, and be patient.

DIY Media Relations

In April 2009, Steve Strauss—the small business expert at *USA Today*—wrote an article called "Should Entrepreneurs Twitter? Uh, No."[4] At the time, Twitter was barely a household name, but many business owners had found success using the social network to connect with people around the globe and compete with larger competitors.

In the article, he detailed the four reasons entrepreneurs should not use Twitter. We had case studies to prove all four of his reasons wrong, and we carefully and thoughtfully commented on his piece. What came of that comment was a phone call where he opened his mind to new and different ways to use the social network. What came of that conversation was another article, "Twitter for Small Business...Reconsidered."[5]

Because he's like everyone else—swamped, with little time to listen to pitches—he reads the comments left on his articles to see if there is anything worth revisiting or diving into more deeply. The following is a step-by-step process to create this magic for yourself.

4.   http://usatoday.com/money/smallbusiness/columnist/strauss/2009-04-06-twitter-entrepreneurs_N.htm
5.   http://usatoday.com/money/smallbusiness/columnist/strauss/2009-04-12-twitter-reconsidered_N.htm

1. Choose one newspaper, magazine, or blog that makes a difference in your industry. It can be the *Wall Street Journal* or one of your trade publications. Choose just one.

2. Once a week, comment on one article, blog post, or editorial. If you disagree, fantastic! Say so. But do it professionally. Being negative or criticizing without a solution isn't helpful. Professional discourse is.

3. Hyperlink web-based resources related to your comments. Cite professional journals or your own work. You want to make it easy for the journalist to find your sources.

4. Keep this up.

5. After about six weeks, the journalist will feel like he or she is beginning to know you, and a relationship will begin to blossom. At that point, you can begin your give-and-take relationship. They'll likely take your phone calls or return your emails, if you're smart about how you approach them.

6. Every quarter, add another publication, so you have four that you focus on each year.

7. Don't be afraid to go after the big publications. If your expertise adds value to the stories they're reporting, comment away!

If you are consistent and post intelligent comments once a week, you'll soon have developed relationships with journalists who call on you when they need someone to interview. Yes, it takes time. Yes, it's hard work. Yes, it requires that you keep up with your reading. But it works. Devoting a bit of time toward nurturing human relationships is a hundred times better than sending your company's news release to 1,000 journalists—and not getting a single bite.

6

The Dark Side of Content

Sometimes the longest distance between two points is the shortcut. Orbit Media Studios, a web design and development firm in Chicago, discovered this when they launched a new website for a client who then hired a public relations firm to promote the new site. Instead of writing an original news release, as might be expected, the PR firm simply copied text from the website's home page and submitted it to online newswires.

It was a disastrous blunder. The release was momentarily picked up by thousands of media outlets, but Google identified it as spam and delisted the new site, making it invisible to anyone who searched for the company's name. In one fell swoop, the Orbit client moved deep into anonymity.

It's easy to understand how this happens. The client, very proud of the site's new content—likely something they spent a lot of time and money on—is happy to have the PR firm use it in the news release. After all, it's interesting to them, why wouldn't the rest of the world want to know it?

The problem is not the website, or the PR firm's tactics for that matter. The site was blacklisted because Google changed its algorithm—to flag sites that use duplicate content—to cut down on spam. Because the online newswires automatically post to websites around the globe, there were—within minutes—more than 1,000 instances of the home page content across the Web.

Now listed on sites such as Yahoo! News, *Wall Street Journal*, and Bloomberg, the PR firm reported success to its client. After all, people around the globe were reading the content the client paid a lot of money to create on their new website. But, because those sites have higher authority than the new website—are more well read and wider shared—Google blacklisted the client's website instead of the sites that had the duplicate content.

The natural inclination, of course, is to blame the web firm when your site disappears from search rankings. But it was the fault of the PR firm, not of Orbit, for not understanding the ongoing changes at Google.

The story ends well. This time. Because Orbit has a great reputation for building white hat websites (meaning they do not spam, try to game the system, or work to beat the algorithms), they were able to file a reconsideration request and explain what happened. Google reinstated the website, and all was well.

Many organizations have hired professionals or a PR firm, web firm, or search firm, in the hopes of getting their company on the first page of search results. This is widely considered magic because no one really understands how it works, so many business leaders don't know who to turn to for search engine optimization help. Many so-called SEO experts claim to do it, so businesses tend to hire based on who talks the best game or with whom they have the most chemistry.

Yes, there are firms that will get you results quickly, but they're most likely using black hat techniques, which will eventually get you banned from Google altogether. The white hat techniques work, but they take longer (it's a marathon, not a sprint), so often the decision makers go with a firm that promises immediate results. Human beings, particularly in our 24/7, instant gratification world want overnight success and a quick return on investment; easily frustrated, we tend to forget how long things really do take.

On top of all the white hat and black hat magic, you have constant changes at Google, which creates a very confusing environment.

If you want to better understand how to use on-page optimization—that is, optimizing the content people see when they come to your site—you've come to the right place. If you want to understand off-page optimization—that is, what happens inside your website with things such as meta descriptions and title tags—read anything by Avinash Kaushik (*Web Analytics: An Hour a Day* or *Web Analytics 2.0*) or Matt Cutts ("Gadgets, Google, and SEO"). They are both Google employees and are very transparent about how all of this works.

For on-page optimization, though, you can learn from the PR firm's mistake. First, understand that Google creates algorithms not only to cut down on spam, but to bring you the very best search results. Their goal is to provide you with results based not only on how you prefer to consume your media on the Web (that is, text, audio, video, or images), but also on what your friends and family read, like, and share online.

Imagine, if you will, a world before duplicate content bans, and algorithms that punish black hat techniques. You type "organic chicken dog treats" in the search bar and up pops a story on Bloomberg about treats that are not only organic and made of chicken, but also sourced in the United States. The second search result is a story on Yahoo!, but when you click on it, you see it's the same story as Bloomberg. You hit your back button and go to the third result, which is the *Wall Street Journal*, but again, the same story.

Not only are all three the same story—they're all written like a traditional news release. Finally you come to a company that *sells* organic chicken dog treats. You click on that, but the information on the home page is the same as the first three links you clicked.

Are you frustrated? Did you get the information you wanted? Do you want to continue reading? Are you ready to quit?

Google wants to prevent this from happening. They measure what is called authority—the influence of the site—and place high-authority sites at the top. If Bloomberg has more authority than the organic chicken dog treat website (which is fairly likely), the news organization's website will come up first and the company's website will be pushed further down.

In some cases, that could be a good thing. After all, if Bloomberg is writing about organic chicken dog treats, most searchers will take that as a credible source and want to learn more. Even better if the Bloomberg article has a link to the company's website. Not so great when the Bloomberg article is the same as Yahoo! and the same as the *Wall Street Journal*.

This is where your PR firm or professional comes into play. Instead of the old technique of blasting a news release on the newswires, media relations professionals today have to be more targeted and specific to the mediums they're calling on your behalf. If Bloomberg has higher authority than the organic chicken dog treat company and they're a top media target, the media relations professional would call (or email, or tweet, or Facebook-message, or send a telegram or a carrier pigeon to) the appropriate journalist there to get a story written for their audience. It would be specific to Bloomberg and not the same story the other outlets are running. Instead of duplicate content, you will have three different topic-specific, exclusive stories written by all three newspapers. These stories might all very well show up before the company's website in search results—but the important thing is they link to the organic chicken dog treat website.

Now the organic chicken dog treat company has some great publicity *and* links from three highly influential websites, which the search engines love.

We talked about white hat and black hat search engine optimization in Chapter 2. While the PR firm that used the company's website copy in their news release is likely not a black hat firm, they lacked the online digital knowledge that, today, is necessary to succeed without hurting one's reputation.

If they had, instead, written a news release that was newsworthy *and* something journalists and bloggers would have been happy to use because it told a story, and pitched it to journalists without submitting to online news directories, the company would have enjoyed many backlinks to its site from high-authority websites, which would have pumped their Google juice, not the penalty they instead received.

Remember, what's interesting to us doesn't always make the news. But if a story is told with passion, a protagonist, an antagonist, a revelation, and a transformation, it's more likely a journalist or blogger will pick it up, do some more research, and write their own, unique story around it. A much better scenario than the same news release running in more than one thousand places.

This isn't intended to scare you, only to help you understand how the Web works and what Google considers a good website. It's a hard nut to crack. The black hat firms still exist, trying to game the system, and now there are also "content farms" that charge very little to "create" content for you. What they are really doing is copying and pasting content off other sites and posting it on yours.

Google will blacklist you for this practice.

In Chapter 1, we spent a good amount of time on how to tell your company's story, examples of stories told well, and how to break down the structure so you can understand what will make your customers care.

But to tell that story to your prospective audiences—locally, regionally, nationally, or worldwide—you have to understand how Google works.

Content Farms and Robots That Write

In February 2011, Matt Cutts wrote on his blog, "In the last day or so we [Google] launched a pretty big algorithmic improvement to our ranking...and we wanted to let people know what's going on. This update is designed to reduce rankings for low-quality sites—sites which are low-value add for users, copy content from other websites or sites that are just not very useful."

In other words, if you use content that is not your own or is low-value (meaning no one is reading it or sharing it), they're going to put a mark against you in their book. If you get too many marks, your site will be blacklisted.

By now, you're convinced you're going to create interesting and compelling content that is your own and is valuable to your reader. So you don't have to worry about getting marks against you for the content you're creating.

You do, however, have to worry about content farms. Imagine a universe where every letter, punctuation mark, word, sentence, paragraph, and page is a commodity. No longer is it about writing copy that is interesting and compelling. It's about who can write the most words in the shortest time. If those words have lots of keywords in them, all the better. Writers are paid not by technical, valuable, educational, or interesting content, but based on the number of words.

For example, a sentence could read: "Another passenger of the vehicle has also been announced to be dead." Or: "Like many fans of the popular 'Jackass' franchise, Dunn's life and pranks meant a great amount to me." Or like this comment, left on a Spin Sucks blog post by "veterinarian website design": "Nice video sharing. It is really useful to me. Please keep posting."

To an amateur eye, these sentences might look okay, but they were written by robots or nonnative English writers. These examples show how quickly the value of your content can be compromised if outsourced to a content farm.

It's not just organizations working hard to create new content consistently that are turning to content farms to pump out copy. Massive news sites such as CNN and AOL have participated in this practice. They use headlines and keywords to trick you into clicking, so you end up on ads paid for by unsuspecting companies that buy banner ads on major sites. Makes sense for them, right? The more clicks they get to an advertiser's ad, the more they can charge.

But it's not all done on the up-and-up. The *New York Times*[1] reported, "These prose-widgets are not hammered out by robots, surprisingly. But they *are* written by writers who work like robots. As recent accounts of life in these words-are-money mills make clear, some content-farm writers have deadlines as frequently as every 25 minutes. Others are expected to turn around reported pieces, containing interviews with several experts, in an hour. Some compose, edit, format and publish 10 articles in a single shift. Many with decades of experience in journalism work 70-hour weeks for salaries of $40,000 with no vacation time. The content farms have taken journalism hackwork to a whole new level."

The good news is the Panda update from Google stopped some of this madness, but there are companies still finding their way around it.

Recently, in a meeting with a group of business leaders, the topic of content creation came up. An attendee said, "I'm thinking about hiring a firm out of India to write my blog posts. They're charging me very little for many posts…and it's cheaper than hiring anyone in the United States. What do you think about that?"

Without saying to him, in front of 600 people, that it was the dumbest idea ever, questions were raised to better understand if his site was mainly for native English speakers, if he had an editorial calendar, and whether he intended to sprint to higher search results, or was prepared to run the marathon. It turns out he was more interested in the sprint; in his words, "I'll just open a new site if Google finds out."

If money grows on trees and you can afford to start over and build a new reputation every time Google changes their algorithms, it's not a bad way to go. For the rest of us, though, content farms are the business equivalent of fairy dust.

The People Who Steal Your Content

As if content farming wasn't enough, there are people who do what's called "content scraping"—which means they'll take the content you've created and post it, verbatim, to another site. This, of course, has the potential to hurt you immensely if you don't monitor it and take action. It's fairly easy—though sometimes laborious—to find out where your content is being used without your permission.

---

1. http://opinionator.blogs.nytimes.com/2011/06/26/googles-war-on-nonsense

Why would someone do that if it doesn't help their search rankings? Some do it based on the assumption that increasing the volume of pages on their own sites is a good long-term strategy, regardless of the relevance or uniqueness of that content. On Spin Sucks, we see all sorts of sites scraping our content: shoe companies, a Japanese textile company, job seekers boards…it's not relevant, but they think it will work in the short term.

As it turns out, Google is very tuned into this practice, so they'll look at the two pieces and decide which one is more valuable. When someone has scraped our content, we have a policy to always comment on their piece (though it almost never makes it through moderation) so they know we know they stole our content. Recently we had someone scrape our content, but it was on a site where it made sense to keep it. Our content director wrote a private email to their webmaster and asked them to link to the original article. They did and apologized for not having done so before. This allows Google to see that Spin Sucks is the source of the original content and, because of the high authority of our site, the search engines rank our content first and the republication of it later in search results.

We point such people to the words straight from Google: "Purely scraped content, even from high-quality sources, may not provide any added value to your users without additional useful services or content provided by your site; it may also constitute copyright infringement in some cases. It's worthwhile to take the time to create original content that sets your site apart. This will keep your visitors coming back and will provide more useful search results for users."

Examples of scraped content include sites that copy your content verbatim and post it without adding any original thinking or value, or sites that copy your content, modify it slightly, and republish it without a link to you as the original source.

There are many reasons someone might steal your content, and often it's done out of plain old ignorance. Perhaps it's a young professional who is just told what to do and, when you point it out, is mortified and very eager to fix it. Perhaps they're inexperienced, or they work for a large media conglomerate that needs to fill many, many web pages with tons of content. But others are more malicious about it.

Some do it because they get paid by the number of visitors they get to their site. Those people will use your content to bring traffic to their site because it's well written, well optimized, and valuable for humans to read. For those reasons—and because you've done all the work—content scrapers want your content on their site.

Others do it for lead generation. You'll see lawyers and real estate agents do this quite often. They want to be industry leaders in their small communities, but most are with clients all day so don't have the time to produce new content. That said, most don't know the content on their sites is scraped content. They have typically hired someone for a minimal amount of money ($30–$50 per month—less than a daily latte!) to "produce" content for them—and that's how it's done. The moral of *that* story? If it's too cheap to be true, it likely is. If you're paying very little for content, you can almost guarantee the people you've hired are practicing poor business ethics and your website, while it may gain some short-term results, will eventually be penalized or, worse, completely removed from search results.

Other scrapers claim they want to create a site full of interesting content, wisdom, and knowledge, but what they're really doing is selling ads to unsuspecting buyers based on the number of visitors to the site. If you bring it to their attention that they have stolen your content, they typically reply with, "I did it to help the community here." But you'll find there is no community—no comments, no social shares—and the site is plastered with ads. But they have the analytics to show they have "visitors" so advertisers buy from them.

There is one incredibly tedious, but effective way to find out if your content is being stolen: put your title into a search bar and see what comes up. If you produce new content once a week, it's pretty effective. You can do that as soon as the day after your publication date and up to a week later. Most scrape almost immediately because their programs are looking for specific keywords.

For sites that produce content daily, though, that's a lot of work. An easier way to keep an eye on things is to add at least one internal link in every piece of content you produce. Let's say you are writing a white paper about new EPA regulations. Somewhere in that content, you want to link to something on your site: a product page, a service page, the contact page, or the request-a-quote page. This creates what's called a trackback. When someone else decides the white paper is really good and they don't want to spend hours creating something similar, they'll scrape your content and put it on their site. The trackback, then, creates a link that sends you an email saying your content is mentioned on another site. Click the link and voila! You've found the stolen content.

A more advanced way to track is to go into your Webmaster Tools (available for many sites), go into the menu, click on Search Traffic, and then Links to Your Site. This shows you who links to you the most, the content most linked to, and the anchor text (or keywords) people are using when they link to your site. Like putting your title into a search bar and seeing what comes up, this process is also tedious, but it's recommended you do it at least once a month to see where your content is being used. The more content you create, the more often it is stolen. It happens to everyone. Be aware.

Manage the Content Scrapers

Now you have to decide what you're going to do with the people who steal your content. You have four options: do nothing, make them aware you know but don't require they remove it, kill it all, or take advantage of them.

The do-nothing approach is the easiest by far. Unless it looks like you've personally endorsed the site that has published your content, it doesn't hurt to just let it be. If you're practicing good content creation with valuable and educational information and people are sharing it on the social networks, the search engines will understand your site is the authority on the topic. It takes a lot of time to fight off the scrapers, and if you've installed the tools that automatically add "this originally appeared on

XXX site" at the end of scraped content, you won't be hurt in search rankings. Tools such as Yoast (a WordPress plugin), FeedBlitz (an RSS feed and email subscription service), and Genesis (a WordPress theme) automatically create that sentence for you so it appears any time someone scrapes your content.

That said, if your site isn't yet considered an authority in your industry by Google, it's worth taking some action against the scrapers.

The "make them aware you know" approach is the most time-effective option. Most sites have places where you can comment on your stolen comment. You can comment with a simple, "Hmmmm…looks familiar." Or, "I'm so happy you liked my content enough to steal it. For those of you reading this, I wrote this for my blog, *YOUR URL*. This is not original content to *SITE NAME*."

If there is no link back to your site, ask them to provide one. If they don't, you can move to the "kill it all" approach.

This approach is a bit more laborious. Sometimes it's as easy as contacting the scrapers and asking them to take the blog post or article down. You can do that either by commenting on the content or by using their Contact Us page. If neither of those exists, you have to get crafty. This is where it gets challenging. You want to file what's called a Digital Millennium Copyright Act, or DMCA, complaint with their host. To figure out who their host is, go to www.who.is and look up their website by typing in the URL of the site where your stolen content resides. That will tell you who the contact is for the site and where the site is registered (GoDaddy, Bluehost, Hostgater, Network Solutions, and so on). Most of the domain registrars have complaint forms on their sites, so start there. If that doesn't work, file it directly with Google[2] or Bing.

The kill-it-all approach works, but you have to be extremely diligent in pursuing anyone who steals your content. You also have to rely on the search engines to take care of it, which renders it a less effective approach.

Which is why you could move to the hardest approach—but also the most fun, if you're so inclined: the "take advantage of them" approach. There are three things you can do to really make content scrapers look silly: internal linking, getting creative with your RSS footer, and installing Yoast (if your site is on WordPress).

We've already talked a bit about internal linking. This is where you add links to another piece of content already published on your site in the new content you're creating. Perhaps you are writing a blog post about how to generate sales leads and you have a webinar that goes into more detail about the topic. Link to the webinar in your new content. Now that you've linked to something else on your site, when someone scrapes your content you automatically receive an email saying that someone has mentioned your site in a blog post or article. Click on that link to be taken directly to the page where you are mentioned. From there, you can determine if the content has been scraped and what to do about it.

---

2. https://support.google.com/legal/troubleshooter/1114905

Probably the easiest and most effective way to take advantage is to use a plugin that alerts you when your content is stolen, and automatically inserts the "this first appeared" sentence. Most content scrapers do so through your RSS feed, so you need to install a plugin that attaches to that.

You can do this through the Yoast plugin—it's already set up this way by default, so you don't have to change anything—or through the RSS Footer or the Anti-Feed Scraper Message plugins. You can even get creative about what that message says, if you want. For instance, some people like to promote their products to those who subscribe to their content, so they will add banners of information about what's coming or what's new. If someone steals their content, the banner also shows up on the offender's site—so now, not only do readers of that site know the content was stolen, they also know you're the authority on the topic and they see your ad for your new products: a webinar, an e-book, a blog series, a podcast, a video, or a sale on a product or service.

Plain Old Plagiarism

Unfortunately, there's more.

On the blog www.thegivegive.com,[3] author Jeff Riddle describes how he discovered that the UPS Store was scraping his content. The third-party writer the UPS Store hired to help with content was using the ideas and tips from Riddle's blog posts, but changed them just enough to look original.

He says, "I found an article on the UPS Store site that was a near replica of an article I'd written as a guest post for the Salesforce blog."

His title was, "How to Grow Your Business Through Client Referrals." The UPS Store title was, "Using Customer Referrals to Grow Your Business."

In his blog post, he had four subtitles:

- Give more value than your clients pay for
- Let your clients do the selling
- Say thank you!
- Process follows culture

The subtitles on the UPS Store were:

- Exceed client expectations
- Empower clients to become brand evangelists
- Always say thank you
- Create a culture of appreciation

---

3. http://thegivegive.com/lessons-for-ups-store-how-properly-plagiarize-so-dont-caught

But it didn't stop there. His content read, "People are naturally motivated to share things of value with their friends and associates, but only if they have something worth sharing."

The UPS Store content read, "It's only natural that people are motivated to share valuable experiences with friends and associates."

The scraping continues throughout the post. Upon further digging, Riddle discovered that the writer for the UPS Store was also copying from other sites. Once the UPS Store was alerted to the plagiarism, they quickly took action.

The formal letter from their PR department read, "Thank you for bringing this important matter to our attention. The UPS Store relies a third party vendor to provide much of the content for our blog, and this news came as quite a surprise to us. As a leading resource for the small business community, we take this very seriously and have since removed the blog posts in question from our site, which were all found to have been written by a single author. We are also seeking new content providers for our blog moving forward.

On behalf of The UPS Store, I apologize and want to assure you we are doing everything in our power to correct this issue."

The best way to deal with unethical writers is to use sites such as TurnItIn or Copyscape that can do a quick scan of the Web to see if anyone has taken your content and revised it to make it look like their own.

Safely Syndicating Your Content

There is one last issue to think about in content creation: syndicated sites. There are major blogs and news sites that use repurposed content. For instance, Bloomberg and *BusinessWeek* "borrow" content from one another consistently. PR Daily uses content previously posted on the blogs of PR professionals, including Spin Sucks. The Huffington Post and *Harvard Business Review* both have content that is published on their sites and on the author's blogs or websites.

In these cases, you'll typically see a line that says, "This content was originally posted on *XXX* site" with a link to the article. This tells the search engines this is not the original source of the content, but they have permission to publish and distribute it. While the search engines may rank both sites, sometimes they'll rank only the original site or even only the secondary site. That depends, in part, on which site has more authority, better optimization, or more social shares, as well as on more sophisticated algorithmic metrics. More importantly, the sites that do use recycled content have more original pieces than not.

You want to be very careful if you syndicate, though. Google will always show the version they think is the most appropriate for users, which may be the syndicated site and not yours. This is okay once in a while because there are other benefits (increased traffic, more subscribers, new audiences, a link from a high-authority site), but you don't want that to happen every time. So, rather than allow an automatic pull of your content to the syndicated sites, set it up so you can manually tell them which content you want them to share.

When anyone uses your content, make sure they include a link back to your original piece. Ideally, they should use a noindex meta tag to prevent search engines from indexing their version of the content, which will leave your content as only one that ranks in search results. If the site has a high authority, you can worry less about the noindex tag; but if your site has higher authority than the site that wants to syndicate your content, insist on the noindex tag.

Be picky about what you allow others to use and what you don't. Some good candidates for sharing include: older content that needs a good revision, new links, and some fresh ideas; a really popular piece that could use a second wind; or a keyword-rich (but not stuffed) piece you know will help your potential customers find you, even if it's on another site that links to you.

It'll be hard at first. As you create new content, Google begins to rank it, and people begin to share it, you'll have bigger sites with high-authority numbers approach you to use your content. You'll be excited to have the extra audience and you'll be flattered someone else thinks it's good enough to run on their site. That's okay. Let them use it.

When you get a request or want to approach a site about using your content, use Open Site Explorer to get the stats on their authority. For example, if you type in `huffingtonpost.com`, you'll see they have a domain authority of 99/100 and a page authority of 96/100. This is very, very, very good. You want to target sites with a domain authority higher than 50 or 55.

Let's look at an example. Say you do recruiting for a living—either you own a company or you are a recruiter. You want to find a site or blog to share your content with, to help with all the things that come from being generous—more traffic, new audiences, brand awareness, or a link from a high-authority site.

Go to Technorati and type in `recruiting`. Change the button in the search bar from Posts to Blogs, then press Enter. There is only one high-authority site that comes up in two pages of search results—A Hire Calling—so this part of your job will be pretty easy. Now go over to Open Site Explorer and enter their URL. You'll find their page authority is 55/100. Not too shabby. They'd be considered a medium-authority site, but one you want to get to know.

To finish your research, go to their blog. You'll discover it's a career blog and not one focused on recruiting. So now you need to decide if their audience—those looking for a job—is the same as your audience. If it is, set about building a relationship with Heather Huhman and see if there is an opportunity to share content. Perhaps she'll even write a blog post for you and later use it on her own site.

The point is, it doesn't matter what industry you're in or what type of content you create. By using Technorati and Open Site Explorer (or any new tools that have been created since the writing of this book), you can find websites and blogs with high or medium authority to help you grow your audiences.

III

Your Brand;
Your Customers

7

Your Customers Control the Brand

Steve McKee, the founder of McKee Wallwork Cleveland, a *BusinessWeek* columnist, and the author of *When Growth Stalls* and *Power Branding,* says that your customers—not you—control your company's brand.

Think about that for a second. Fortune 500 companies spent millions of dollars and multiple years on fancy advertising and run huge global PR campaigns to tell their customers and prospective customers what they want them to think about the brand. If someone was happy, they didn't tell anyone; if they were unhappy, they would tell 5 to 10 people, and maybe write a nasty letter to the CEO—a letter that almost always went unanswered.

Now, with the speed of the Web and the immediacy of social media, customers tell not just a handful of people but thousands if they're happy or unhappy about doing business with you. That's good and bad. It's good if they're happy, but if they badmouth you online on a moment's notice, you have to be paying very close attention. Most hope you're paying attention and will address their issue immediately—while others simply want to tear you down.

Let's start with the good. Twitter, Facebook, YouTube, Instagram, and Foursquare are changing the way business happens, whether you're a company leader or a consumer. Let's say you have a retail location and one of your brand loyalists checks in on Facebook Places or Foursquare (both are location-based tools that link to a person's online network of family and friends). That person's 500 friends see that and, having never heard of you, wonder why their friend is there, and probably ask about your store. Suddenly you have new customers because one loyal customer checked in—they told their friends—and their friends told their friends, and so on.

But what if your organization doesn't have a retail location? What if you build your business through word-of-mouth and referrals, and not from foot traffic or in-store sales? It's a little more difficult to use the social networks to build awareness in this case, because people can't "check in" when they visit. Customers can, however, tell their friends and family about you through the same social networks—and you can encourage it.

Perhaps you're at a trade show and you want people to tweet about the new product they just saw in your booth. Encourage them to tweet about it, using your Twitter handle or a hashtag that defines your business. For instance, imagine you just picked up a copy of this book at a conference. A tweet could be, "Just got a copy of #spinsucks at the industry conference." Or, "Grab a copy of #spinsucks to better understand PR for your business."

As you can see, it's very valuable when your customers or clients tell your story for you. They sing you praises, they become your advocates, and they even stick up for you when you make a mistake.

Now, the bad. In early 2009, Skittles took a risk and prominently displayed its social networks on the home page. Instead of the usual "me, me, me" copy on the brand's home page, it featured their corporate Twitter stream, their YouTube and Flickr channels, and their Facebook fan page. Today that seems like no big deal, but at the time, it was very innovative and interesting. After all, they were pretty much handing the keys to their home page over to customers, allowing them to say whatever they wanted.

On the first day, they had so many hits to their home page, it took down Twitter and its servers. And then, just two days after its launch, the marketing team had to rethink its strategy when users deluged the site with inane and profanity-riddled tweets. It became a game, in fact, to see how ridiculous a user could be with their social posts, and still end up on the Skittles home page.

It was risky and it failed, succeeding only in educating the world about the importance of controlling brand images. Today, the Skittles site still prominently displays their social networks and provides updates on what is being said about the brand online, but it does so in a way that supports the brand positioning.

While you can help motivate your customers to talk about you in a good way, ultimately they are the ones who control the message. Your canned messages are no longer enough. Yes, the things you, your executive team, your sales team, and your employees are saying about the brand should be consistent. But you also have to listen to how your customers describe your organization, your products, or your services. If they perceive it differently, it's time to rethink your messaging and your brand positioning.

On top of the new way of thinking about how you communicate your brand's promise, you also have to consider how quickly a mistake you make can be told online.

Understand What Your Customers Think About You

A startup called Belly Ballot created a contest to pay an expectant mom $5,000 to let the Internet name her baby.

Natasha Hill was having a hard time deciding on a name for her unborn child, due in a few months. She also wanted to wipe clean her credit card debt and start saving for her child's college tuition before the baby was born. So she entered a contest to let total strangers name her baby.

The catch? She only gets the cash if she actually gives her child the name the Internet voted most popular. The blogosphere was all up in arms about it: "A real mom wouldn't let complete strangers name her baby!" and "Quick! Someone, get her a baby name book!"

It turns out the blogosphere was right. A real mom *wouldn't* let complete strangers name her baby. Natasha Hill was an actress hired by Belly Ballot to create publicity (and that they did, starting with *The Today Show* and growing into *New York Daily News*, *BuzzFeed*, MSN, and blogs galore) and she wasn't even pregnant. Nope. Not pregnant. It was a hoax.

When asked why they did it this way, founder Lacey Moler said, "We came up with the idea for the contest, and we knew it would be controversial. We're a startup, and we wanted to control the situation. We never thought it would get this big."

The founders seem like genuinely good people who had an interesting idea for a company and just wanted it to succeed. Their naivety about how the media works led to their demise. For most startup organizations, having a communications expert on their board is advisable. It's unlikely this was a malicious attempt to manipulate the media.

The other mistake they made was in trying to "control the situation." They started by creating a contest that no one entered. So they decided to give it legs—and provide a real story to media outlets—by naming a winner. Only they didn't have a real winner, so they hired an actress. And give it legs they did. If it had been real, the publicity they gained for their startup would have been invaluable. But they chose an unethical route because they wanted to control the situation.

There are a few lessons you can take from the Belly Ballot Hoax.

1. **Nothing beats hard work.** Creating a fake contest, announcing a fake winner, and not thinking about what will happen if you get caught is the wrong way to go about things. There isn't an easy button. By doing it this way, Belly Ballot quickly undermined the trust they had managed to build and guaranteed no one will want to cover their story for a very long time.

2. **You can't control the situation.** If you're going to grow a business, you have to use the Web to do it (not necessarily social, but the Web), and you can't control that. Instead, control your operations, your culture, and your talent. The rest will come.

3. **Social media is unkind.** If you lie, you will be found out. Every time. It isn't like the old days where it would take years for someone to figure out what's really going on. With all the information we have at our fingertips, you will be found out quickly, and your story will spread like wildfire.

4. **If there are no entries, there are no entries.** There are plenty of contests that just don't fly. It may be your first instinct to hire someone to play a winner. Don't! It's not ethical, it's not right, and the publicity you'll gain won't be worth the bad publicity you will have to manage when you're found out.

5. **Always be ethical—to a fault.** Honesty is the best policy. Don't create whisper campaigns about your competitors, don't lie to journalists and bloggers, and don't create something out of nothing.

You no longer have control of your brand. The truth of the matter is, you never did. You only had the perception of control because you didn't hear the negative things customers were saying. If customers left, you could only speculate as to why. You ran your business in a vacuum.

Now you have a great opportunity to not only understand what customers think about your brand, but to change the way you do business to support them. And it is an opportunity. This isn't scary stuff. It's a change in how we think, in how we do business, but it's a huge opportunity. Many of you have competitors who have taken the bull by the horns, while others work in an industry that still faxes job orders. No matter which bucket you are in, the opportunity you have in front of you is great.

Communications Done Well

In January 2013 OXO, an innovative consumer products company that makes Good Grips and other cool kitchen and laundry tools, was accused by one of its largest competitors of stealing designs from some of their inventors.

The competitor, a company named Quirky which has offices down the street from OXO and whose CEO knows OXO's CEO fairly well, took to the streets with billboards, as well as employees holding up unflattering signs in front of the OXO offices. Instead of calling the OXO CEO to discuss the issue, the competitor made it very public. Human beings love a good fight, so it quickly became a movement spreading through both the online and offline worlds.

Not one to take it squarely in the jaw, though, OXO wrote an open letter to their customers.[1] It began, "Earlier this week a consumer products company located two blocks from OXO started a very public campaign accusing us of stealing a product idea. After thoughtful consideration, we decided that we needed to clarify the situation. It is not our practice to defend ourselves publicly. In fact, this is the first time in the history of our company we have ever taken a public stand like this. But sometimes, you just need to set the record straight."

---

1. www.oxo.com/quirkyresponse.aspx

They go on to tell the story of how Quirky accused OXO and their design partner, Smart Design, of stealing a feature from a product called the Broom Groomer, which was submitted to their community in 2009 by an independent inventor and launched in 2010. Their product includes "rubber teeth on the back of the dustpan [that]... quickly and easily comb out dust bunnies."

The story continues by explaining where rubber teeth on dustpans come from, dating clear back to 1919 when Addison F. Kelley applied for—and received—a patent for the very thing. His patent expired in 1936, and, to this very day, when a dustpan has a "teeth" feature, it is relying on that patent.

They then explained—directly to Quirky—how the inventor community works, showed some photos of product features the company seems to have stolen from OXO, and talked to the people who submit ideas through the Quirky crowdsourcing platform.

This is a great example of communication done well, for six reasons. They weren't defensive, their response was well researched, it engaged customers both personally and emotionally, it was educational, it was fact based, and it was timely.

1. **Not defensive.** It's human nature to get defensive in situations like this. Perhaps this wasn't the first draft, but what eventually came out was laid out very well and not defensive in the least. In fact, it's so calm and level headed, you can almost hear someone telling you this story, dare we say bedtime story?

2. **Well researched.** They describe the story of the "rubber teeth" inventor and then go on to show images and captions of features Quirky uses in their products that are similar to OXO. Their only point? Everything is derivative of something else—there are rarely new ideas, only new ways to use what already exists.

3. **Personal and emotional.** While they did not get defensive, they still were able to hit your emotions by describing how the Quirky offices are only two blocks away from them, how some of their employees know one another, how their leaders run in the same circles and have spoken before. They appeal to your emotions by asking, "Isn't it a little strange Quirky didn't think to pick up the phone and call first? Wouldn't that have been the right thing to do?"

4. **Educational.** By reading this, you receive a great lesson on how patents and inventions work in the real world, and on what you should consider if you submit an idea to a company and they end up using it.

5. **Fact based.** The letter is long, but they were very careful to tell a story based on facts. They cited 13 sources so as not to leave the argument up to chance.

6. **Timely.** It took OXO four days after the first Quirky billboard went up to issue this letter. While that may seem like an eternity in today's fast-paced digital world, because it was so well researched, it worked.

When Quirky responded, it was none of these six things. It was written (and posted) quickly, and it came across as extremely defensive: "We do not plan on further engaging in a tit for tat open letter writing campaign." Whether or not this would have legs in court is another thing, but in the court of public opinion? OXO wins.

Your Customers Are Active and Passionate

When bin Laden was captured and killed, when the plane went down in the Hudson River, when the bombs went off at the Boston Marathon—how did you get that information?

Think back to when the plane went down in the Hudson River. It was January of 2009, and it was when Twitter became a household name. A man named Janis Krums tweeted, "There's a plane in the Hudson. I'm on the ferry going to pick up the people. Crazy" (Figure 7.1).

Figure 7.1 *Janis Krums tweets about the plane in the Hudson River and becomes a household name.*

With that tweet was a picture which the traditional media used in nearly every story told around the globe (Figure 7.2). Krums was the first "journalist" to the site, and he scooped the story. His photo shows the people getting off the plane, onto the wings, and into the lifeboat—something the news media wouldn't have been able to capture. He told the news far more quickly than anything we had been accustomed to.

Fast forward four years to April of 2013 when bombs went off at the Boston Marathon. How did you learn about that news? Now think about later that week when the manhunt for Dzhokhar Tsarnaev was under way. Were you glued to the television screen? Did you have the radio on? Or were Facebook and Twitter open all day as you waited with bated breath for the outcome? How did you get the information?

Perhaps you went to work and didn't pay much attention until you got home. Or maybe you were completely obsessed. During the manhunt, it was very possible to have the television running in the background, while following updates on Twitter and Facebook, and listening to the police scanner. In fact, the channel on the police scanner that people around the globe were listening to was eventually shut down, because officials were fearful Tsarnaev was following the updates people were posting on Twitter and staying a step ahead. Though they asked time and time again for people

Figure 7.2   *US Airways flight in the Hudson River. The photo was tweeted and then used globally in news stories.*

to stop updating the social networks while listening, it was impossible for them to control the situation.

When you look at your own behavior—how you get your information, where you participate online, where you read your news—you can tell things have changed. But, for some reason, we want to hold on to the idea that we have control over how people perceive our brands.

Customers are now in control. They control how they interact with your brand, what they tell their friends and families (which could be hundreds of people with their own social networks) about your brand, and even how they give you information about their experience with your brand. Sometimes it's annoying, and other times it's pretty enlightening.

Recently, a blog reader asked us how to tell who wrote each blog post. We told her the author's name and bio information is at the bottom of each blog post, if you visit the blog online. It turns out, she only reads the blog posts in her email and the post's author and bio don't appear there. Because we spend all of our time on the online blog, we had no idea of what is visible to those who do not read online. We added a simple one liner to the body of each blog post about the author, and had several comments that it was a helpful change. Enlightening.

Glenn Platt and Peg Faimon are codirectors of the Armstrong Institute for Interactive Media Studies at Miami (Ohio) University. They look at this phenomenon as part of their research. "We have become an economy of makers and doers," they say. "Today's consumers are not passive; they are active in their brand enthusiasm and passion. It's about doing things. Today's consumer does not want to be told what to think about a brand . . . they want to be able to tell the brand what they think."

From your perspective, how do you interact with the companies where you buy your favorite products? Maybe it's the grocery store, a new piece of technology, a rental car, appliances or a hotel or restaurant. If something goes wrong, what's the process you use to let the company know?

Remember the Avis story in Chapter 4. When we had a bad experience, we first tried customer service on the phone. When that didn't work, we moved to Twitter. When that didn't work, we changed our rental car company. Have you had a similar experience?

It doesn't matter if you are Nordstrom and claim exceptional customer service, or Bob's Party Hats and claim one-of-a-kind party hats—the experience your customers have with you should be the same in person, on the phone, online, and on your social networks. If it's not, they're more than willing to express their disappointment with you—and your brand.

Your Brand Is How Customers Feel About You

Your brand—how it appears, how it makes people feel, what it *says*—is what you want your customers and prospective customers to think about your organization. Your brand is you. It's what you lie in bed thinking about at night. It's what Tony Hsieh, the CEO of Zappos.com, did when he envisioned a business with superb customer service and a culture everyone was excited about. It comes through in your messaging, in your website content, in your social media activity, at the trade shows, when you speak to audiences, and in your internal meetings.

If your branding, however, doesn't match what people—both internal and external audiences—feel about your brand, things can go off the rails.

In today's 24/7/365 digital world, brand development happens constantly. It's an ongoing, two-way conversation between an organization and its customers. You introduce new products or services and begin the conversation. Your customers respond and react—sometimes very vocally and sometimes more quietly. You respond and refine based on what they're saying. It's hard. Sometimes you feel very defensive—but even Steve Jobs, who was famous for saying, "I don't believe in market research," had to refine based on customer feedback when the iPhone 4 had cellular connection problems. In 2010 he admitted, "We're not perfect."

That said, the rules of branding have not changed. The tools have changed, and the way we get feedback has changed, but the idea remains the same. A small handful of organizations approach branding with deliberate conviction. Apple, Nordstrom, Zappos, and Whole Foods are a few that come to mind immediately. These organizations stay focused on their vision and their brand no matter what roadblocks are thrown in their way. They maintain focus, discipline, and execution. Everything they do supports customer service, culture, innovative products, or the environment. They have brand stewards, loyalists, and ambassadors. On the flip side, though, they have critics and bullies who try to find an experience that doesn't match the image they're building. They know how to harness both groups, how to tweak and refine based on feedback, and what to ignore.

Most organizations, though, have a scattered approach to branding. Most don't know what they're trying to achieve. Some want to be all things to all people. Some don't have specific niches. Some don't have a clue at all. No one cares about these brands. Not only do you have to have something to work toward, you have to give your customers a reason to care, good or bad.

While you can't control what people say about your brand, there are some things you can do to help shape perception.

1. **Be vigilant.** Not just in repeating your brand message over and over again, but in monitoring and listening to the conversations happening online about you, the company, your products, your services, your competitors, and the industry. Today we have such a great opportunity to know exactly what people are saying about us. Harness that information, be vigilant about paying attention, and use it to massage your messaging, tweak your offerings, or even create new products.

2. **Be honest.** You're going to continue reading this, but remember: "I'm sorry" works wonders. If there is a product issue, be honest about what is happening. Keep people updated. Communicate the ups and the downs. When you're honest about any issues, challenges, or concerns, there isn't a story to tell. People are willing to forgive. It might be painful at first, but the pain won't last as long as it would if you lie or attempt to sweep the problem under the rug.

3. **Be open.** This one is so hard. It's difficult for human beings to keep open minds about many things. When your company, your product, your service, your employees, or even your policies are under attack, it's really hard not to get defensive. But if you show a willingness to talk about issues, and even change your policies based on feedback, you'll create the most loyal customers.

4. **Be active.** Many business leaders think they have to jump on the social media bandwagon and have accounts on all of the social networks. That just isn't true. If your customers and prospects aren't on Twitter, for instance, why would you spend precious resources there? That said, it could very well be that your customers use Twitter for personal reasons. Maybe they follow celebrities, watch for deals, or lurk to get the news, but they don't tweet or engage in conversation unless they have a customer service concern. If you're being vigilant about listening to the conversation, you'll see them tweet about you, even if you don't have a Twitter account. Be active in responding to that and be open to the feedback they provide.

5. **Be consistent.** Many organizations don't know who they want to be when they grow up. Their employees all deliver different messages when they attend trade shows, when they meet someone on an airplane, when they blog, when they tweet, or when they go to networking events. Remember, the rules haven't changed—only the tools have changed. Figure out what your vision is, create your elevator pitch and supporting messages, and train everyone to use them. The way your organization is described should be consistent—through every single person who works for and with you. After all, if you aren't consistent, how can you expect your customers to know who you are?

6. **Be creative.** Not every person who complains about you online will deserve a response. And not every complaint will be solvable. But if you're creative in how you handle those things, other customers and prospects will see that and appreciate the effort. There is a sandwich shop in New York that had a bad review. One bad review. Someone posted on Yelp anonymously that the sandwich they're famous for was disgusting and uninteresting. The next day, the sidewalk chalkboard sign in front of the restaurant said, "Stop in and try our daily sandwich. The one @djinto thinks is disgusting." Not only did that encourage people to stop in, it made rounds on the social networks. People love a sense of humor and creativity.

7. **Be proud.** Once you figure out your vision—what you want to achieve, who you want to be when you grow up—post it everywhere. Create plaques for employees to hang over their desks. Have a sign made for your entryway. Include it on your website. Some organizations even include it in their email signatures. Eventually people will get accustomed to seeing it, and no one will have any doubt about where you are going. Be proud of what you are doing and don't be afraid to tell the world about it.

Pay attention to what your customers are saying about you online. Participate in the conversation. Listen to their wants and needs. Let them help you with customer service, new products or services, and market research. Let your customers tell their friends about your brand. And stop thinking about controlling what they say about you. Control is out. Empower is the new black.

IV

Spin Sucks

8

The Convergence of Media

In late 2011 and early 2012, the Public Relations Society of America undertook the big task of redefining public relations. Before this happened, the industry was working with a definition that was 30 years old. It hadn't been reviewed since 1982.

A lot has changed since 1982, but more so in the past decade. Social media has completely turned the PR industry on its head, and technology is changing more quickly than ever before.

Consider how long it took some of the things we use every day to reach 50 million users:

- Radio: 38 years.

- TV: 13 years.

- The Internet: 4 years.

- iPod: 3 years.

- Facebook added 100 million users in just 9 months.

- iPod app downloads hit one billion in 9 months.

Nearly every year we have a new social network introduced: Google+, Pinterest, Instagram, Vine, SnapChat, Whisper. The list continues to grow. It's not only the job of communicators to keep up, it's your job as business leaders to stay abreast of the changes so you can lead your team in the digital age.

Technology is creating amazing opportunities for all of us, but also causing some distress. You used to have a PR team (internal or external) focused on employee communications, media relations, reputation management, financial reporting, the annual report, public affairs, and maybe some events. Today, PR professionals have to be knowledgeable about web development, mobile marketing, search engine optimization, content marketing, and more.

The Web is extremely important in the job of a PR professional—much more important today than it was in the previous decade, as new technologies are being introduced and companies are struggling to figure out how to add the latest and greatest tool to their marketing strategies.

It used to be your website was an online version of your corporate brochure. But times, they are a changin'. Your website now needs to be a living and breathing document that changes consistently (at least once a week, according to a HubSpot study[1]) and becomes less about you and more about your customer.

The best place to start is your website, and the first thing you can do is *take out the French* (the we, we, we). Your website must provide the WIIFM—what's in it for me—for your customers and prospects.

You have paid media (advertising), earned media (media relations), shared media (social and community), and owned media (content housed on your website and blog). Owned media is great because, if you can write in an engaging and conversational way while adding value, you no longer have to depend on media buys, influencers, and journalists to tell your story for you. You can do it yourself.

The Convergence of Media

In 2012, The Altimeter Group released "The Converged Media Imperative: How Brands Must Combine Paid, Owned, and Earned Media."[2] It talks about how three of the four not only integrate but affect the role of the PR professional. The premise behind this research is the same in *Marketing in the Round* (Que Publishing, 2012).

The Altimeter report says, "Consumers distinguish less and less between paid, owned, and earned media, yet marketers remain specialized in one medium at the expense of the others. Rather than allow campaigns to be driven by paid media, marketers must now develop scale and expertise in owned and earned media to drive effectiveness, cultivate creative ideas, assess customer needs, cultivate influencers, develop reach, achieve authenticity, and cut through clutter."

Since the release of this report, shared media has become its own beast and joins the fold with the other three media. But the concept remains the same. As business leaders, you have to think about how your customers interact with your products or services,

---

1. www.hubspot.com/lead-generation-tips
2. www.altimetergroup.com/research/reports/how-brands-must-combine-paid-owned-and-earned-media

how they integrate, and how to continue to grow your organization—and your customer base—with the new tools available.

It's not easy, which is why not everyone is doing it, but organizations that don't figure out how to effectively converge the four media types are at a huge disadvantage.

We are all consumers, no matter how or where we buy. If your business doesn't sell to the mass consumer, that doesn't mean your customer isn't a consumer. He or she buys the same way from you as you buy from Apple or Coke or Starbucks. But in a business-to-business organization, you have a huge advantage: Many of your competitors have not yet discovered the convergence of media, which means you have an opportunity to take the market lead and you get to learn from the good, the bad, and the sometimes ugly mistakes of the business-to-consumer organizations.

What this means is, as you converge your media efforts by combining social, content, advertising, and media relations, you can connect with your customer *no matter where they are.*

Let's say you manufacture the food the big box retailers put in their freezer sections under their own brand name. Your customer is not the shopper because your brand name isn't on the box. Your customer is the person who buys the frozen food for the grocery store, and you have to communicate with every grocery store chain in North America.

It used to be your sales team would go on the road, sit in the lobby at the headquarters of each of the chains, wait hours to be ushered in, and then be given 15 minutes to talk about why your macaroni and cheese deserved to sit behind the label of the retailer. Rinse and repeat. Day after day. But then the Great Recession hit, and not only did you have to reduce the travel budget for your salespeople but the retailers laid off people, which meant your contacts either were without jobs or were doing the jobs of three additional people.

Then they began hiring new college graduates, who were tasked with finding macaroni and cheese at the lowest price…and were incentivized to do so. Those young professionals took to the Web to find the manufacturers, learn about their company and the products they make, and negotiate price. All without ever looking into the whites of a salesperson's eyes.

At the time, many manufacturers didn't have websites allowing for this kind of investigation from the retailer, so the buyer went on to the next company. And the next and the next, until they found what they were looking for. The buyer never picked up the phone. He or she never invited your salesperson in for a visit. You were lucky if you received a personal email, but most likely you received an email through the form on your Contact Us page. If you didn't respond within 24 hours, the buyer marked you off his or her list.

Today, the buyer is looking for more than just a website. They first do a search to find the companies they want to investigate, then they Google your company name. They rank you, based on what they find. Do you have a Facebook page, do you have a Google+ account, does your address pop up in Google Places, do you have a blog, have you or anyone on your executive team been interviewed and does that show up in search results? They are looking for a convergence of how you use all of the media to determine whether or not you're credible.

Sure, you still do business the old way. You still have customers who prefer to see the whites of your salesperson's eyeballs before they sign on the dotted line. But those customers are retiring, and the new buyers will do business exactly as just described—no matter who you are, what you sell, or what your reputation was before the digital age came.

By no means should you put this book down and get your organization on all of the social networks, start blogging every day, and hire a bunch of people to run your digital media as it grows into a beast you can't manage. There needs to be strategy, positioning, and an understanding of your customer to figure out where on the Web you want to participate. But you no longer can have a website that is six or more years old as your only web presence.

Today you have to think about how the four media types converge—not only to have a presence on the Web, but to own the online space in your industry. Owned and earned media are vital to your business. They build the brand, garner credibility, and amplify your messaging. Paid media has always led marketing initiatives because it's more tangible than owned or earned. You can hold and feel it. Your friends and family will see an ad on TV and call you to say they loved it. It leads online and offline tactics, but it can no longer be used alone because it doesn't work like it used to, not without being bolstered by the other media. And shared media helps your customers find you no matter which device, screen, or media they're using.

Because your customers distinguish less and less between the four media, your entire livelihood will, in the very near future, depend on how you drive effectiveness, cultivate creative ideas, assess customer needs, build relationships with influencers, develop reach, achieve authenticity, and cut through all the clutter that is out there, competing with you for the same top spot.

On-Page SEO for Your Content

In Chapter 3, we talked quite a bit about owned and earned media—their definitions, how they work, and what types of content to create if you're set on implementing an owned media program.

What we didn't discuss, however, was how content works in search engine optimization and how to integrate it with the other media forms. We also didn't discuss how to use the hard work you've done on your vision, messaging, positioning, and target audience preparation in your four forms of media. And we didn't talk about how to integrate all of this to celebrate brand ambassadors and turn critics into fans.

Let's do that now.

It used to be you'd have to hire a PR firm to tell your story for you. They'd use the relationships they had with journalists, TV and radio producers, and other media to gain third-party credibility for your organization, product, or service by working to develop a story—or a series of stories—about you. While it's still valuable to do that if you are concerned with brand awareness, thought leadership, and credibility, you have a huge opportunity to create content that can also build a groundswell where your top-tier journalists are calling you instead of the other way around.

Owned media is the content you create for the things you own: your website, your blog, your collateral, your brochures, even (in some cases) the things you post on the social networks (though you don't totally own it and it can go away if the network dies).

But the difference between the content you used to create for those things and today's definition is that they have to be valuable and interesting to your audience. They cannot be all about you. They need to highlight your thinking, your process, and even (in some cases) your intellectual property.

HubSpot did a State of Content Marketing survey a few years ago. In it, they asked 1,400 business owners how content affects lead generation for their organizations.

The results were interesting. Of the business-to-consumer organizations that consistently create new content, 88 percent had generated more leads than before they began content-marketing. Among business-to-business organizations, 67 percent garnered more leads.

The survey also found that the more content the organizations created, the better their inbound lead generation was. Respondents had:

- Ten percent more leads if they created one or two new pieces of content per month

- Thirty percent more leads if they created two to four new pieces of content per month

- Seventy-seven percent more leads if they created more than four new pieces of content per month

Though the study isn't recent, its results are still relevant for content in lead generation. Content is the newest form of marketing right now, and organizations that haven't yet taken advantage of it have a huge opportunity before them.

What Is On-Page SEO?

On-page search engine optimization (SEO) is what you do to the text people see when they read your website, your blog, or any of your online content. Once upon a time, SEO was all about what happens on the backend of your website—meta descriptions, title tags, and links were all the rage. But then Google discovered the search experts were gaming the system, and they changed the rules.

Now, as you learned in Chapter 2, Google wants to see really good content that has keywords inserted in a way a human being would actually speak. Before, companies used what is called *keyword stuffing*. A search expert would take a word or phrase they wanted to rank for and put it in a piece of content as many times as they could. This would alert the search engines they were relevant for that topic and the page would be returned at the top of search results.

The problem? It tended to read something like this:

"I've always wanted to be a fairy princess. If I were a fairy princess, I could snap my fingers and little fairy princess elves would clean my house. Little fairy princess elves would paint my toenails and fairy princess elves would brush my hair. My laundry would be done by fairy princess elves and the fairy princess elves would cook my dinner. The fairy princess elves would make me chocolate cake every night and the fairy princess elves would make me homemade ice cream."

That was painful to write, let alone read.

How Does On-Page SEO Work?

In January of 2013, Google released its 24th version of Panda. The goal of Panda is to return only high-quality search results from sites that have high authority. So, if you want to rank for "fairy princess," you have to be smart about how and where you place that phrase throughout your copy. If you write it like above, not only will you not rank for the phrase—Google will slap your hand by pushing you down in the search results. Now you have to think about:

- Content of the page
- The title tag
- The URL
- The images' alt texts

Content of the Page

Write content that makes human beings happy. Not only should it be valuable, informative, educational, and engaging; you have to write so search engines can understand you have authority on the topic, without overkill. You can use any combinations with your phrase; in this case, we'll use combinations with "fairy princess."

"I've always wanted to be a **fairy princess**. I would sit in my library every morning and read some books while my elves tidied up my bedroom and made my bed. Then I would move to the patio, where the sun would warmly welcome me to my **fairy**

princess chair. There I would write about the handsome prince who would someday find me and sweep me off my feet. We would have scads of children who are raised to believe in their very own prince or **princess**."

You want to have at least 300 words, but 500–700 is magical. In a 500-word piece of content, you might have some variant of "fairy princess" five or six times. The three times in the few sentences above is a little too much—one phrase every two sentences is a lot—but you get how it works now. Think about how you can incorporate your phrase without overkill.

The Title Tag

If you write in a content management system (WordPress, Blogger, Joomla), you can create title tags without having to go into the programming side of things (Figure 8.1). The title tags are also called headings. For instance, the headline above ("The Title Tag") is what is called an H3, or third-level heading.

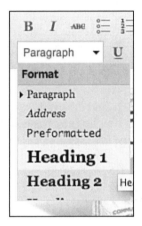

Figure 8.1 *An example of where to find title tags in a WordPress website.*

The URL

Have you ever noticed a URL on your own site that reads something like this: `http://www.companyname.com/123456`?

This is bad.

What you want is this: `http://www.companyname.com/fairy-princess`.

This is good.

The keyword or phrase should always be in your URL. If you're using WordPress, it's easy to change by clicking on the Edit button next to the permalink at the top of the post. Just copy the headline, paste it there, and voila!

The Images' Alt Texts

Every piece of content you write should have an image. After all, people are visual learners so you want to give them something to look at that helps break up the text. When you insert a photo or image into your content, the system will let you provide what is labeled Alt Text (Figure 8.2).

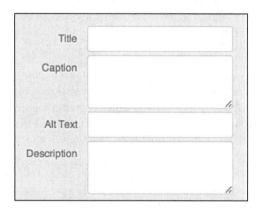

Figure 8.2   *An example of how to change the information on an image to help with SEO.*

You'll see title, caption, alt text, and description. You really only need to worry about the alt text. Copy your headline and paste that into that box, too. That will associate the key phrase with the image.

Tools to Use

There are plenty of tools you can use to help you with on-page SEO, but a favorite is Yoast. It attaches to your content management system so you can see blank boxes when you open a draft post or page. It gives you a red, yellow, or green light based on how well you've optimized your content.

If you have a red or yellow light, it makes recommendations on what you can do to fix the page. After you make changes and click Save Draft, it changes the color for you until you're at a green.

Shared Media Through Community

Now that you are progressing through owned media, it's time to share all of that content you've created.

In the early days of social media, everyone talked about community. Build your community. Talk to your community. Community is the bee's knees. Everyone should have a community.

Speaking from the perspective of having one of the most active communities in the PR and marketing world, that is hooey. Yes, community is important, but if you think about it only from an engagement point of view, you will be angry you spent so much time and energy building it.

But let's back up and talk, first, about what community *means*. Mitch Joel, the author of *Six Pixels of Separation* and the new *Ctrl Alt Delete*, wrote a blog post a few years ago about building community. He said you don't have community until the members begin to talk to one another without the help of the author or moderator.

And he's right. The magic happens not when you begin to get comments on your content, but when those people begin talking to one another. This isn't something that can be created or forced. It happens organically. But there are things you can do to help the community grow and encourage members to begin building relationships with one another.

The secret sauce is this: There is no secret sauce. However, if you spend some time talking online to the people who can influence purchase decisions, you can provide the foundation for your community. And, when you do it this way, it becomes much more than engagement. You build a virtual sales force that isn't on your payroll. You build goodwill. You build trust among a group of people who will go to bat for you in a crisis. You build a referral network. And you build relationships with human beings who will not only buy from you, but will become your biggest advocates.

Think about it from this perspective: Just like you, prospects, candidates, customers, journalists, and bloggers want to be noticed. They want to know their comments or content resonates. They want you to acknowledge it, share it, and help their voices be heard. Help them do that.

With people who spend their time with your content, visit their sites. Comment on and share their content. Follow them and engage on their social networks. Publicly thank them for their efforts.

For journalists and bloggers, visit the sites of those who you want to notice your content. Comment on and share their content and begin to build a relationship that way. Respond to people when they comment on your blog. Visit their blogs. Comment on their blogs. Share their content. Give them a reason to want to visit you—again and again.

This is hard work. You're building relationships with human beings. That doesn't happen overnight. But it's worth all the elbow grease.

Exactly *how* worth it depends on your goal. More than likely, your goal is not only to build brand awareness and gain credibility but to increase sales. So how will you use your community to do all of those things?

There are a few things you can do immediately to massage the community.

- **Install Livefyre.** Livefyre is a commenting platform for your blog or website that allows people to not only comment and engage with one another but follow the discussions via email. While some of the other platforms do something similar, Livefyre is more user friendly—it provides many different options for readers to set their settings in a way that's convenient for them.

- **Answer comments.** There is a big debate in the blogosphere about whether or not you should respond to comments. Many journalists and bloggers believe the article or blog post is their say and the comment section is for the readers to agree or disagree, but not for the author to participate. If, however, you are trying to build community for the sake of increased sales, it is imperative the author speaks to the people who are commenting. After all, you can't build relationships—online or offline—by sitting in your throne and not speaking to the people.

- **Engage people with one another.** This is another thing Livefyre allows you to do. Just like on many of the social networks, you can "tag" people in the conversations. By using the @ button, you can type a person's name and invite them to the conversation. They'll be alerted either on one of their social networks or via email and follow the link to extend the conversation.

- **Introduce readers to one another.** We do this through our weekly #Follow-Friday blog post. Every Friday, you are introduced to one member of our community, which provides information about professional and personal lives, including hobbies, interests, and fun facts we've learned about them while they've hung out with us. This provides an opportunity for members of the community to get to know someone they see in the comments a little bit better. Rumor has it there have been many in-person meetings, many friendships formed, and even some dating among the Spin Sucks community. While that doesn't do a lot for direct sales for us, it certainly creates a deep loyalty that is tough to break.

Your customers. Your community. The influencers. The journalists. The bloggers. All of these people will help you grow your business. It's no longer about just the people inside your organization—it's also about those outside. Some will buy. Some will refer others to buy. Some will talk about you nonstop. Some will talk about you only once or twice—but when they do, it's powerful.

These people distinguish less and less between the four media types, which is why the convergence is here to stay.

9

Crisis Communications: Trolls, Critics, and Detractors

Applebee's, the restaurant chain, found itself in a pot of hot water when a waitress was fired and the community lashed out. The characters are: a guest, two servers, and Applebee's Facebook page. The *Mercury News* sums up the situation well: "A waitress at a St. Louis Applebee's lost her job for posting online the receipt upon which a pastor had declined to leave a tip, with a snarky note saying she gave God 10 percent. After her dinner on January 25, Pastor Alois Bell crossed out the automatic 18 percent tip charged for parties of more than eight. 'I give God 10% why do you get 18,' she wrote above her signature. Employee Chelsea Welch—a colleague of the stiffed server—took a picture of the receipt and uploaded it to the online site Reddit. She subsequently lost her job, an Applebee's spokesman confirmed to TheSmokingGun.com, for violating a customer's privacy" (Figure 9.1).

The issue here isn't whether the server should have been fired—if your policy is such that employees are not to publicly discuss your guests, then the person should have been fired. The issue isn't a debate between leaving a tip or not. The issue isn't even the rage people felt as they took to the Web to demand that the waitress gets her job back, creating "Rehire Chelsea Welch" groups on Facebook.

The issue is in how Applebee's responded. After the receipt was found on Reddit, Applebee's was forced to communicate their side of the story. Around 3 p.m. on the day after the server was fired, Applebee's posted a note on their Facebook page, shown in Figure 9.2.

That should have been the end of the story. They communicated their policy of protecting guests' personal information, how the guest was treated, and what happened

Figure 9.1   *Copy of receipt, as posted to Reddit, shows a pastor stiffs a waitress of her tip.*

Figure 9.2   *Applebee's stirs the pot by posting their side of the story on Facebook.*

to the server who posted the photo of the receipt. Unfortunately, the social Web won't let things die if they can prove you wrong. There is a funny meme you'll see reappear every once in a while of a man on a computer with his spouse behind him tapping her foot. The caption reads, "Just a minute, honey! Someone is wrong on the Internet!"

And that's what happened here. Not willing to accept the formal status update, the Internet went to work. They found an image—on the same franchisee's Facebook page—of a guest's personal information that was posted just a few days prior (Figure 9.3). Of course, this is great feedback—something we would all love to publicly post on our websites or social networks. But, according to Applebee's, their policy is not to ever publicly share a guest's personal information.

So the questions began. "Why wasn't this person fired?" "How can this still be on your page?" And a comment war on the company's Facebook page ensued. The photo was screengrabbed, and people began to share it to prove the hypocrisy and double standard of the company's policy.

Figure 9.3 *Back of a receipt where an Applebee's customer praised the service he received.*

The criticism and negative comments continued throughout the afternoon, into the evening, and through to the middle of the night. Around midnight, the comments really began to take steam and whoever controls the Applebee's Facebook and Twitter streams began commenting to people with the same preapproved message. They simply copied and pasted their message over and over and over again. Not only was it the middle of the night but they got extremely defensive, let emotions rule, and forgot one important thing: Social media is *social*.

They posted the preapproved message as a comment, instead of another status update, and with thousands of comments it quickly got lost in the shuffle. So the person continued to copy and paste the same message in response to anyone who said anything defamatory against Applebee's. And, because the statement was impossible to find, the person handling the account began to tag the people who were commenting.

Copy and paste cold message. Copy and paste cold message. Copy and paste cold message. This went on and on until people began calling them out for managing the critics in that way (Figure 9.4).

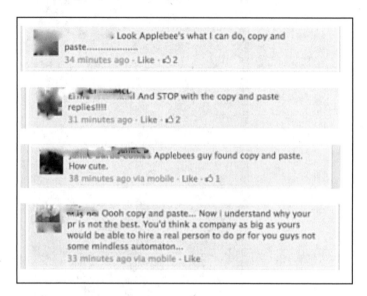

Figure 9.4   *Applebee's creates a bigger social media crisis by copying and pasting a preapproved message (rather than posting it once as a status update), and people don't like it.*

This debate continued until about 5 a.m., accumulating hundreds of thousands of comments that were not complimentary to the brand. To add to the pain, the company has a widget on their home page called "What's the Buzz" that anyone visiting the site—with or without a social media account—can see. That widget updates instantly with tweets from customers (Figure 9.5).

In this real-time, instant gratification world, it's important to stay on message. It's easy to get wrapped up in emotion. It's easy to want to defend yourself. It's easy to put logic aside. But those are the things that will make the issue worse. Every time.

But it also creates some real challenges—challenges that used to be reserved only for organizations that have highly risky products (oil, gas, chemicals) or those with unethical or fraudulent employees. Crisis communications used to be a profit center inside a public relations firm. Now every communicator has to have crisis expertise.

Figure 9.5 *What's the Buzz, a widget on the Applebee's home page, shows critics of the brand.*

People do stupid things. People get fired. People make mistakes. We're all human beings. It's in how you handle the issue that makes all the difference in the world. In fact, the difference between an issue and a crisis is how it's handled. The terms *issue* and *crisis* are often used interchangeably, but they're not the same. Certainly they share some characteristics: Both can be damaging to your business, both can originate internally or externally, and both must be managed. Most importantly, though, both require a communications expert (or team) to provide a careful, completely thought-through strategy.

What happened with Applebee's was that they reacted. They weren't thoughtful, they didn't think through the consequences of debating commenters in the middle of the night, and they (seemingly) were too inexperienced to handle the outpouring of negative sentiment created. Instead, they got defensive and made things worse.

The difference between an issue and a crisis is you rarely hear about the former. Crisis examples abound: Susan G. Komen, Penn State, and Carnival Cruise Lines. All of these organizations had someone inside the organization who did something wrong. Those were issues. But, because the executives at these organizations either ignored them or failed to act swiftly and decisively, those issues became crises.

Don't assume that if an issue isn't public knowledge, you are scot-free. Quite the contrary, in fact. The more time passes, the harder it is on the organization when the issue is discovered…and it will be discovered. It always is.

Consider Penn State for a moment. Let's say the school fired Jerry Sandusky as soon as they discovered what was happening—and it sounds like they discovered it many,

many years before it came out. What would have happened? Yes, there would have been negative fallout. Sure, parents may have been apprehensive to send their sons to that school for a year or two. But in the long term, Penn State would have been perceived as taking quick and definitive action against a predator, protecting not only their students but children in the community, the football program, and the university. Joe Paterno wouldn't have had to retire in shame, his statue wouldn't have been removed, and the issue would have been a small footnote in the school's history.

Instead, the organization swept it under the rug, hid it for as long as they could, hoped it would go away—and when it didn't, faced a crisis that could last for generations.

Another example is Tiger Woods. When the story broke about his marital problems and multiple affairs, the golf professional went into hiding. In February 2010—three months after the car accident that broke the story—Tiger Woods held a news conference to apologize to his fans, sponsors, and the golfing community. It was scripted, he read it while sounding disjointed and discombobulated, and he sat alone on the news podium without the benefit of having his family next to him.

Three months of speculation. Three months of tabloids trying to find him. "We think that is Tiger in a hooded sweatshirt leaving a sex addict clinic!" Three months of pure conjecture only to end with his reading a script in front of a camera and not taking any questions. He would have been better off just recording a video and releasing that.

Sure, there are some who think this is a nonstory—that it belongs to Tiger and his family. But, just like an organization or a product, Tiger Woods is a brand. With that comes a responsibility through the media to his fans and sponsors. The extramarital affairs, the car accident, the more than furious wife...all of that is an issue that can be managed by holding a news conference immediately after the story breaks. It didn't have to be anything more than, "My wife and I are having marital problems. We are working with a counselor to try to save our marriage. We ask you to respect our privacy during this time."

While that wouldn't have prevented anyone reporting on it or the tabloids speculating like they do, it would have been confined to a 48- or 72-hour news cycle instead of three months of creating news out of nothing.

A contrasting example is an organization that acted swiftly and appropriately: Domino's. In 2009, a video made by some employees hit YouTube in quite a flurry of activity. The employees filmed themselves spitting and sneezing in food and then serving it to customers. They uploaded the video to the Web for all to see, sending it to friends and bragging about their prank.

The company, upon finding this video, not only fired the employees, but their CEO made a public apology in front of a camera, which they then uploaded to YouTube. The franchisee whose employees made the video also created a video apology and offered discounts or free pizzas to current customers. The corporate office and the franchisee used their social networks to amplify the message, made sure their apology was heard, and offered a solution to be sure this didn't happen again.

It created immediate trust because it was handled within days—not months—of the employee's video release.

Applebee's = crisis. Penn State = crisis. Tiger Woods = crisis. Domino's = issue.

Managing an issue requires communication. It should be strategic, thoughtful, and targeted. If Penn State leaders had taken steps to fire Jerry Sandusky years ago, the university would have needed specific messages for its board, shareholders, managers, students, parents, teachers, community, and the media. It would have had to have been carefully planned; there would have been several hours long, late-night meetings as the communications team (made up of executives, communications experts, and lawyers) thought through every possible scenario. By doing so, they could have framed the story to show how an institution such as Penn State would not tolerate such actions and how they took immediate steps to hold those responsible, accountable.

When you're managing an issue so it doesn't become a crisis, it's important to remember that often, it's not the content of the story that matters, but who tells it first. When you tell your story, you have the best opportunity to stay in front of it. Take the punch to the nose. It may break, but it will heal.

When the media finds out about your issue and they tell their story, you almost always end up with a crisis. Once your issue becomes a crisis and makes the headline news, there is no way to answer what you knew, when you knew it, and what you've already done without looking guilty in the public eye. Wouldn't you rather be the one in control of that message?

Tips for Managing an Issue

Act swiftly. Domino's is a great example of how a company acts swiftly to manage an issue so it doesn't become a crisis. That said, it took them a few days to react—which, in today's 24/7 information age, is a lifetime, but when they did react, it was masterful.

You may not think you'll ever have an issue to manage. Perhaps you sell capital equipment or professional services or product packaging. Surely your organization doesn't have any issues. It used to be we'd create crisis communication plans for clients and they'd sit in desk drawers for an entire year until we reviewed and revised them. Today, however, the social Web creates an environment where you have to be on your toes all day, every day. An employee could say something racist online. A customer could have it out for you and spread lies through their Facebook page. A competitor might engage in a whisper campaign against you. The only way to win at the game is to be prepared, have a communications expert on your team (or have one on speed dial), and act swiftly. Not in a week, not in a month, not in three months—on the same day.

Address the problem. It's not fun to have to come out and say you screwed up or something bad has happened. In fact, it kind of sucks. But it's the only way to prevent a crisis. It's amazing how two little English words work as well as they do: "I'm sorry."

Not "I'm sorry, but…"—just "I'm sorry." When you address the problem head-on, you have the opportunity to tell the story from your point-of-view, to say you're sorry, and to provide solutions. Think about this in your personal relationships, maybe the heated arguments you've had with a friend, spouse, colleague, or partner. What happens if you just say you're sorry instead of trying to win the debate? There is a funny word that the *How I Met Your Mother* characters, Lilly and Marshall, use during an argument. It is "pause." That means, "I'm still angry with you, but we need to take a step back." In their TV relationship, it works as well as "I'm sorry." It immediately defuses the situation. You feel better, your partner is no longer mad, and things go back to being fun again. It's the same thing in business: We screwed up, we're sorry, and here's what we're going to do to make sure it never happens again.

Communicate the story. A story gets out of control when you haven't told your side of it and people begin to speculate. With Tiger Woods, the tabloids were speculating he was going in and out of a sex addict clinic (he wasn't) because he hadn't told his side of the story—so they began to make things up based on what little information they had. This is extremely damaging to your brand. While you can't control the story, you can provide the facts, information, and access to executives that allow journalists and bloggers to help you frame it in the right way. Likewise, Ann Curry's departure from *The Today Show* was covered in-depth by *The New Yorker* magazine. It delved into whether or not Matt Lauer orchestrated the whole thing. It was a fair and balanced and really well-researched article, but what was missing was Curry's side of the story—because she refuses to talk about it. The story was published more than a year after the fact, and the media were still speculating about what happened from Curry's perspective, because she won't communicate the story. Wouldn't you rather tell your side of the story than have someone else tell it for you, mired in speculation?

Communicate where it happens. As we saw in the Domino's example, if an issue or crisis is exploding on YouTube, that is where you go to diffuse the bomb. Their CEO recorded a video and posted it on YouTube so it would come up in searches when people were looking for the original employee video. Of course, it was then shared through other social networks and embedded on the company's website, but it lives on YouTube. If the story is unfolding on Facebook, that's the tool you'll use to tell your side. If it's happening in the more traditional media, that's where you'll focus your energies.

Hire a communications expert. This shouldn't be someone who knows how to use social media or someone who works for a company that has experienced an issue or crisis. I'm talking about someone who has deep and intense experience in managing an issue or crisis. Typically these people work in PR firms and specialize in crisis communication or reputation management. It's unlikely a company will go through enough issues or crises in its lifetime to give anyone employed within the expertise you'll need if something happens. If you can't afford a communications expert, become BFFs with someone who can help you think through issues when they arise. Put them on your advisory board. If you have a paid board, add them to that. Have that person on speed dial. In the Applebee's example, it's pretty clear the person behind the avatar didn't have any communications experience. Though it's never been admitted to publicly, an educated guess says that person was young, had been out with his or her friends (it was a Friday night, after all), got home, saw the Facebook stream lighting up, and decided to engage the commenters. Someone with crisis expertise would have known how to minimize the blowout while watching intently so he or she could counsel the executives the next morning on steps to take.

Think before you act. Yes, things happen in real time. Yes, we live in a 24/7/365 world. Yes, it's fast paced and you have to act quickly. But that does not excuse you from *thinking*. When we were kids, my dad used to tell us all the time, "Don't ever put anything in writing you don't want used against you later." Have you ever been so angry that you wrote an email, press Send, and later regretted it? Rather, write those things, let them sit overnight, and then delete them. It makes you feel better, and there is no damage done because it never sees the light of day. It's the same thing with an issue or crisis. It will be emotional. You will feel defensive. If it will make you feel better, write down what you really want to say and then delete it (*please* delete it—or it will eventually find its way into the wrong hands!). It's corny to say this, but time really does heal. Sometimes all you need is a communications expert, an attorney, or a business adviser to vent to—and then you can go about the task of communicating rationally and without emotion.

Empower your team. Lululemon is an athletic clothing store. They mostly sell yoga wear, but also have nice running attire for men and women. Early in 2013, it was discovered you could see through some of the women's yoga pants, creating a very expensive situation for the company. They had to recall the pants from their stores and offer refunds to women who bought them. Not only did they have some fun with the issue—a window at a store in Vancouver had a sign that read, "We aim to be transparent"—but they empowered their team to do what they thought was best for each individual customer. Because of it, the story fanned out fairly quickly, and it became a case study in how to manage an issue the right way. Let your team help. Set the expectations and boundaries, give them the tools and resources they need to be successful, and let them at it!

Say I'm sorry. This bears worth repeating. Of course, you have to mean it and it can't be accompanied with the word "but." When you practice saying "I'm sorry" in your everyday communications, it becomes easier to say it—and mean it—when an issue develops.

Back down when you're wrong. If you hold a position on something and someone points out there is a double standard or you're being hypocritical, reassess your policy. For instance, Applebee's said they have a policy against disclosing a guest's personal information, which is the reason they gave for firing the waitress who posted the pastor's note and name. But people soon found a positive note, with the guest's name, on one of the franchisee Facebook pages, proving a double standard within the policy. Rather than admit wrongdoing, however, Applebee's stood behind their policy—they didn't take down the second note or fire the person who had posted it (admittedly, doing that would be going a bit too far). A great message would have been, "You're right. We have a double standard in our policy. The note with a guest's name has been removed from our Facebook page and we're revisiting our policy with each of our franchisees."

Have a communications expert on speed dial. Have someone on speed dial who has lots and lots of experience with issues and crisis management. You might think you'll never need it—and maybe you won't—but Murphy's Law dictates that the second you think you don't, something will happen. It's like having insurance: If you have it, you won't need it.

Begin to Repair Your Online Reputation

There is an interesting thing happening that is brand new to most of the experienced business leaders: Negative reviews, untrue comments, and trolls are pushing their way to the top of search rankings. Now, when someone Googles you, they find all of these negative things said about you online that might be 100 percent false. Or, as in the case of a client of ours, the reviews and comments could be true but you've already changed your operations to address them. Either way, cleaning up your online reputation is now a very real thing—and something just one person can ruin for you fairly quickly.

Perhaps you remember the story of a Florida pizza shop owner, Scott Van Duzer, who hugged President Obama during a campaign stop in 2012. The President stopped by Van Duzer's restaurant to recognize him for his efforts in helping provide blood to patients in his county. What Van Duzer didn't expect was that the big bear hug he gave the President would make national news...and bring out the trolls on his company's Yelp page (Figure 9.6).

People from all across the country began leaving negative reviews on the page, even if they'd never actually eaten in the restaurant. One reviewer wrote, "Most of y'all Democrats can't afford to eat at this restaurant anyway. They don't accept food stamps." Hundreds of anti-Obama commenters flooded the page to criticize Van Duzer, his restaurant, and his political beliefs.

By working with Yelp, Van Duzer was able to have some of the comments removed because they violated the site's content guidelines, yet many remained. But then something magical happened: Van Duzer's loyal customers came to the rescue! They began leaving five star reviews, having actually eaten in the restaurant, and the negative and untrue reviews were pushed further and further down.

Sure, you can still find them and, if someone does a lot of digging, they might hurt that person's perception of the restaurant—but how often do you go beyond page two, or maybe three, of search results?

If there are negative things said about you online—negative reviews, unhappy former employees, critical blog posts—it takes time to clean that up. It's doable, but it's hard work. Anyone who tells you it can be done with an algorithm and a few finger strokes is taking you to the cleaners. Not only is the work they're doing unethical, Google will find out and penalize you—not them—for the shady practices.

Figure 9.6 *Big Apple Pizza reviews on Yelp which were left when the owner gave President Obama a bear hug during a campaign stop.*

The proper process goes a little like this.

Conduct an online audit. Likely you already know what's there, but it doesn't hurt to do a Google search, see what is being said, and where it lands in search results (second listing, first page). Do this both logged into your Google account and logged out (or you can open an incognito window in your browser without having to actually log out). Logged-in results will show you what your friends, colleagues, peers, and clients will see, and incognito results will show what the rest of the world sees. It's important to have both. Search Google, Bing, and Yahoo!. Search the social networks.

Search the review sites. Search the Better Business Bureau and Ripoff Report. Search employee sites such as Glassdoor. Use terms such as "I hate *COMPANY NAME*" or "*COMPANY NAME* sucks."

Also, do searches on key employees or executives at your organization. Look at sites such as Spokeo that aggregate content from all over the Web—including personal information such as a home address—to determine what is out there that you may not like. It's pretty easy to remove your information from Spokeo, but if you apply for a car loan or a new credit card, it's fairly common for you to reappear on those sites. Keeping a watch on not only the company but your name and those of your key employees is something you should revisit monthly.

If you find negative reviews in search results, it's likely someone has created a Facebook page, a blog, or a Twitter hashtag to talk badly about you with other people who feel the same. Pay attention to what they're saying and keep track of it all. It's not always necessary for you to respond, but it is imperative you monitor the conversations. Take screenshots so you have context when you review it in an audit later, and include a breakdown of any and all websites, blogs, discussion forums, and social networks where conversations are happening. Include what you are doing right—and wrong—and compare it to your competitors.

Create a strategy. Based on what you learn from the audit and what internal and external implementation resources are in place, put together the company's online strategy—and make sure it's tied to your goals. The very first thing you should do (if you haven't already) is set up alerts to let you know when someone says something about you online—positive, neutral, or negative. As of this writing, Google Alerts are the most popular way to do this, but there are rumors that the free service is going away. There are lots of alternatives, including Talkwalker. It seems to be a little more efficient than Google Alerts, giving you better information much more quickly.

As you create your strategy, you'll want to think about whether to use tactics such as influencer marketing, brand ambassadors, or customer reviews to help you provide information about the great things you do. The customer reviews are easy: Just ask people to write reviews for you. A good way to do this is to post a sign at the register, include a link to the review sites on your website or blog, or just simply ask for them. The one thing you cannot do is provide incentive for good reviews, such as a gift card or discount on services. That's considered against the rules and will get your page shut down on the review sites.

For influencers and brand ambassadors, think about what types of things you can offer ahead of public announcements. Perhaps it's early access to a new offering, a free product, or special access to a hard-to-reach executive. Whatever you decide, make sure the strategy falls in line with the organization's vision and goals.

Create a cleanup list. With the audit complete and your online strategy in place, now comes the cleanup. In some cases, there will be multiple accounts for your organization. There might be profiles you don't need on social networks that either are defunct or don't help your strategy. There might be negative reviews or blog posts on the first page of search results you'd like to address so they don't come up before your own sites and the positive reviews. Maybe there are "I hate *COMPANY NAME*" groups on Facebook or untrue reviews on Yelp or TripAdvisor. Perhaps former employees have said really terrible things about you on Glassdoor, or they've set up social networks for the company and you don't have the login information. Whatever it happens to be, the list begins with these types of things. Write down everything you need cleaned up so the person or team responsible understands what it is you want done.

As you create the list, read the reviews, comments on blogs and in discussion forums, and all other negative things people are saying about you. Aggregating all of that information into one place will help you decide if your products need to be tweaked, your customer service needs to be enhanced, or your operations need some work, particularly if there are comments about the same things over and over again.

But, more often than not, people just want you to respond to them. They want to be heard. When they post something and it goes unanswered, their fire is fueled. As you create the list of things that need to be cleaned up, make a list of sites where your team should respond to complaints. You will want to create some preapproved messages for your team to use when responding—such as, "I am so sorry to hear about your troubles with our company. If you'll privately send me your phone number or email address, I'll be glad to help you offline." What this does is show anyone else who reads the complaints that you are responsive, but takes the conversation offline where you can be helpful. In the best cases, the person will go back to the site after you've helped them and post how grateful they are for your help.

Assign a person or a team to do the work. They will need usernames and passwords, branding guidelines, sign-off on copy/images, and the power to make changes without a laborious approval process. It's not critical for this person to be in marketing or PR, as long as it's someone who understands what you're trying to accomplish and can get you the information and answers you need in a timely manner. Assign certain people to complaints, others to delete unnecessary social networks or get the login information to those missing, and others to begin a list of content that should be created, based on what people are saying. For instance, as I was doing research for this chapter of the book, I realized Spin Sucks (the blog) doesn't come up in search results for "online reputation management." I added that phrase to my list of content to write in the next few months. If I've done my job correctly, you'll be able to find us when you search that phrase by the time this book is published. You can do the same for the types of things people are saying about you already or things they're searching for and not finding you.

There is one thing you should think about when you assign a team to do the work, particularly for those who are responding to customer complaints. You need to remember they are representing your organization in a very public forum. Just like you'd only send experienced people out to meet with high-profile clients or to a big sales deal, you want your cleanup representatives to have enough business experience to make informed decisions. That's not to say an intern or a young professional who has great social media expertise can't help—they can. You just want those people to be supervised by someone who has the expertise to make the right decisions devoid of emotion and defensiveness. You don't want what happened to Applebee's to happen to you. Combine social media savvy with experience—and you have a great cleanup team.

Begin the cleanup. Some of this is painful because you'll need to work with the social networks' customer service departments to reset login data, delete a profile, or take down an untrue review. This could take weeks. One of our clients had an employee who was very social media savvy. He set up the company on all of the social networks and then quit his job, taking the login information with him. Despite numerous phone calls, emails, texts, and a letter from the attorney, he refused to provide the information. Working with LinkedIn, in particular, took about five weeks to reset the password and provide administrator access. In some cases, such as on the review sites, you have to prove the review is untrue—sometimes with legal action. You are guilty until proven innocent: The social networks and review sites assume you'll say and do anything to take down negative reviews…especially if they are true. You have the burden of proof on you and they'll make you jump through a gazillion hoops to make sure you're telling the truth.

A friend had to sue a former client because of non-payment. When that client received the formal lawsuit, he went on to Yelp and blasted the company. Not only was what he said not true, it was libel. And it kept showing up at the top of search results, which hurt their business during a long six-month period. She and her business partner had to put the lawsuit on hold as they spent months working with Yelp to prove they were not the ones who were the liars. It eventually was taken down, but the cost of lost business during that time was insurmountable.

There are organizations that will charge between $3,000 and $10,000 to start the cleanup process for you. Others charge a flat monthly rate and will do whatever it takes to remove the complaints and negative reviews. But these are just starting points. If an organization quotes you $7,000, for instance, you can almost guarantee they'll come back to you in a month and show you a list of things they uncovered that will coerce you into paying more. I realize I'm biased when I say this, but I prefer to see you do the cleanup and manage your own reputation as part of a larger communications strategy. That said, I'm also a business owner. I'd rather pay for something strategic that will help me get to my long-term vision than for a quick cleanup that may not have lasting effects.

Whichever tack you take, it's not a fun process, but if you really, truly want the cleanup to happen, it's an unfortunate one that you'll have to endure. It takes time and patience, but it works. Remember it's a marathon, not a sprint.

Build your online presence through social media. There was a time when social media didn't make sense for every organization. Now, though, it's the best, most efficient way to connect with your customers and prospects. You have the ability to build relationships with many people at once, versus the one-on-one of the old days. Even for business-to-business or niche organizations, there is now a social network that is applicable to you.

There is one social network every organization should be on: Google+. Not only does Google rank you higher if you use their social network to promote your content, it helps to push down the negative content if it has been shared on Google+ (for more about this, see Chapter 2).

The important thing to remember about the social networks is they are just that: *social.* No one goes to a networking event to only talk about their job. The common flow of conversation includes asking about your family, your interests, your hobbies, and even some of your favorite travel locations. Think about the social networks in the same way. For instance, LinkedIn can include interests and hobbies while Facebook—a place where people go to for a brain break during their workday—can include fun questions, memes, or photos.

No one will want to follow you, friend you, like you, or have conversations with you if you're one-dimensional. Think about it from your own perspective. If you meet someone who can only talk about how great the products are that he sells, you'll run as far away from him as possible every time you see him. The same is true on the social networks. If you only talk about how great you are, no one will seek you out for conversation.

Google now allows you to connect your social networks to your analytics (Google+ is automatically installed; you have to have a programmer to do the others) so you can see not only which social networks are the biggest drivers of traffic to your site, but also what keywords they used to find you, what conversations (or pictures, or links) drove them to you, and what they did once they arrived.

This is important information because it helps you measure your popularity among the people you want to find you. Think about being likeable and fun…and don't talk just about work. If people like you, they will recommend you. Be three-dimensional. Be fun. Be entertaining. It's scary to do that at first, and many of you will think, "Why would anyone care about that?" But they do care. Find out what works, watch your analytics, and tweak along the way.

Content is king…or at least prince. Many of you will have negative reviews that are, unfortunately, true. There are many organizations who claim they will clean up your online reputation for $40 per month, deleting all of the negative reviews from search results. Don't fall for that. It's impossible to delete things on a site unless you have administrator rights. Sure, you can hire someone on their word and take your chances. It's certainly a lot cheaper than hiring a communications professional, but remember: you *always* get what you pay for, and this is one of those instances where—like with a washer and dryer, or a camera—it pays to spend the money.

A communications professional not only understands that content is king, but knows how to use it to push down the negative reviews. He or she also understands there is *nothing* you can do to remove them. The best you can do is push them to pages three and beyond—the pages no one ever visits when they're doing research on your company.

Here's an important thing to note: There is only so much content can do to help your online reputation if your operations are screwy. In other words, if your customer service sucks, or your product is cheap, or your business model is broken, people will continue to complain about you online—and they'll always show up on the first page of search results.

When we work with organizations that have lots of negative reviews, one of the things we always ask is, "Are you prepared to change the way you do business?" If the answer is no, they're not ready for us. If the answer is yes, but they don't actually plan to change anything (this happens more often than not), it'll take about 90 days to figure that out. But if you're really ready, content can help you as you change your operations.

Consistency, value, and education are key when creating content that will move negative reviews down in search results. If you hire a person or a firm who knows what they're doing with content, you have nothing to worry about. If you decide to hire a content farm (which is offensive to me as a writer, but plenty of executives go this route), you have to make sure that

1. The content is yours (in other words, not stolen from another author),

2. The content is valuable to your target audience(s), and

3. The content is educational enough to give a reader, viewer, or listener something they can't get anywhere else on the Web.

When you go this route, you'll have to manage the process more closely and you'll have to constantly search the Web to be certain the content you're getting wasn't scraped from another site. It has happened to very large organizations that spend lots of money on communications professionals but decided that content can be outsourced to a different country. It can happen to you.

Implement the strategy. Once you've cleaned up the organization's online presence and figured out how you're going to use content to build a strong reputation, it's time to put your strategy into action. You're about to become transparent, which is really scary for most business leaders. In the past, we had the perception that we are in control of our reputation even with an issue or crisis (see Chapter 7). The curtain has been pulled back now, and the only way to participate in the conversation is by being transparent: You're opening yourself up to criticism and feedback. This can be pretty painful when you have an organization you care deeply about, but it's necessary not only for having a great online reputation but for meeting your business goals.

Allow employees to talk about your products or services publicly. Establish a one-to-one communication channel where customers can engage and converse with you in real time every day. Proactively ask for feedback. (This one always hurts a little bit. As soon as you ask for feedback, people give it…and it's not always good. But if you can set aside your emotions and really listen to what they're saying, there is often a new product idea or a tweak to a service you hadn't before considered.) And don't hide criticism: address it publicly.

Once you've decided to be transparent, honest, authentic, and human in your online conversations, the content, brand ambassadors, influencer marketing, customer reviews, and a solid product or service will help you cross the marathon finish line.

Warren Buffet famously said, "If you lose money for the firm, I will be understanding. If you lose reputation, I will be ruthless." An organization's reputation, today, is only as good as its search results. If your operations are solid, you have a responsive customer service team, and you run things ethically, the rest will sort itself out.

10

The Future of Communications

It's pretty difficult to look into a crystal ball and predict the future. We might have more luck with a Magic 8 Ball. "Magic 8 Ball, is the communications industry going to continue to change?" That's a guaranteed yes.

Joking aside, there are some things bubbling on the surface we'll see come to fruition in the next 10 years. Things that are guaranteed to happen in that time are self-driving cars, a stagnating education system in the United States, China becoming even more influential economically, people getting sick of information overload and unplugging more often, technology continuing its lightning-fast pace of advancement, and the world of communications continuing to evolve. The lines between communications, marketing, advertising, sales, customer experience, product development, and human resources will become so blurred it will be hard to decipher where each belongs.

Communications professionals must adapt and change, while keeping up with the times. Business leaders must understand what the industry can provide and ask for it, specifically. When you think public relations, it is not longer just about getting your name in print. Media relations is merely one spoke in a larger wheel. Today you must be using communications for brand awareness and credibility, and also as an investment in your organization's future. If your communications team is worth its salt, they will be able to prove the work they're doing is an investment and not an expense.

You'll also see communications play a bigger role in customer experience. To see how that trend is evolving, remember what happened when George Zimmer was ousted from Men's Wearhouse, the company he founded in 1973.

A scrappy entrepreneur, Zimmer took one store in Houston and built it into a multibillion-dollar empire. For as long as anyone can remember, the founder has appeared on television as the front man for the men's clothing retailer. Pretty much everyone in North America can recall his deep voice saying, "You're going to like the way you look. I guarantee it."

Though he handed the chief executive reins to Doug Ewert in 2011, Zimmer remained the company spokesperson and the face of the brand. But in June of 2013, Zimmer was dismissed as executive chairman and subsequently resigned from the board, signaling a disagreement over major cultural shifts in the customer landscape.

Casual Fridays in offices gave way to "we don't care what you wear" every day, high unemployment numbers meant more people were staying home in their pajamas (or workout clothes), and a shift to more virtual environments meant less men were buying suits. It's not a surprise an organization built around making a man's suit more affordable would begin to decline.

When Zimmer was removed from his position, it was implied the disagreement was over strategy, and soon after the company made a $96 million acquisition. It's impossible to know the real story, but what we do know is Men's Wearhouse reported a 28 percent drop in profits the quarter Zimmer was ousted, and the company (as of this writing) continues on its downward spiral.

Phrases such as "stakeholder value" and "market trends" were heard—and read—over and over in the public communications from the company, but there was little mention of customers. The investors who support your business are important to keep in mind, but they don't buy from you. They don't guarantee your growth. They don't tell their friends and family about you. Ironically, they aren't always the best judge of what your customers want.

This is how business has been done, but the distance between numbers and people makes it easier to dismiss what customers really want. It's also hard for employees to get their heads around. Saying "There has been a drop in earnings" is very different from saying "We missed the mark with our customers." Using the word "earnings" signals to employees, "All we care about is making money for the head honchos." Using the word "customers" sends a different signal: "We care about the people you interact with every day. We care about their experience. We care about what they have to say about our product or service. We care about your interaction with them."

It's imperative to understand the market and pay attention to the business results of earnings and shareholder value, but today we must do so by connecting those dots to customers and the very real way they interact with brands.

As the company Zimmer founded tries to find its way, the outside world is seeing changes in the way they communicate. Their social channels are shifting from being all about them, their sales, and their promotions, to a more customer-centric focus through content and conversation. It's a sign they are beginning to realize customers are the only path to profit.

In Chapter 7, we learned your brand is controlled by your customers in the outside world. What they think about you, how they experience you, and how they interact with what you sell is what they'll tell their friends, family, and social networks about. Their voice is unlike anything you've ever heard—and not a single one of them is afraid to use it. Don't like that Zimmer was ousted? They're telling thousands of fans and followers. Love the new suit collection? They're blogging about it to hundreds of readers. Have trouble with alterations in one of the stores? The photos are posted on Instagram and Pinterest.

Movie studios got away with producing terrible movies for a long time. As long as they made a splash on opening weekend, shareholders were happy and moved on to the next project. Now, thanks to Twitter, Facebook, and Rotten Tomatoes, movies can succeed or flop before they even officially open.

Take *Snakes on a Plane* as an example. The Samuel L. Jackson movie about, well, snakes on a plane, generated more online buzz than any movie before it. The campy title inspired parody fan videos and had investors predicting major success. So major, in fact, they predicted it would make $20–$30 million on opening weekend. It opened at $15 million, half of what they expected. While the online buzz generated a ton of earned media (or free publicity), moviegoers immediately reported on the film's shortcomings, and discouraged others from seeing it.

Thanks to our peers, we now have early warning signals on everything from movies and clothes to software and hardware. There is hardly a product or service available that doesn't have an instant review mechanism in place, be it the social networks or something more formal such as Yelp, TripAdvisor, or Amazon.

Customers buy from you, therefore they are your shareholders. The future of communications is to begin treating them as such.

Real-Time Marketing

While the importance of customer experience will continue to grow and organizations will have to figure out how to communicate in the places that are convenient for each individual customer, there is another new trend emerging: Real-time marketing or, to use the phrase *Forbes* has coined, "brand improv."

In Chapter 1, we saw how Oreo took advantage of the lights going out during the 2013 Super Bowl with a quick tweet that said, "Power out? No problem. You can still dunk in the dark." With this very funny—and well-timed—tweet, Oreo quickly became the Super Bowl's social media darling. Brands quickly followed suit—copying the idea, but not executing as well. Timing really is everything.

Several months later, however, Honda upped the game. The car maker launched new TV spots for the Honda Odyssey, which has the world's first in-car vacuum cleaner. The ads feature all the things you find on your car floor. Voiced by Neil Patrick Harris and Rainn Wilson, crayons, candy, lint balls, tiny toys, wrappers, and crumbs animatedly chatter away during the commercial—before getting sucked up by the vacuum.

A creative ad—which is what most organizations would have stopped at in the past—was then coupled with a strong social element. A few days after the ads began airing on television, the Honda Twitter account picked fights with snack and fast food brands' Twitter accounts to promote their new in-car vacuum.

Honda tweeted to Skittles, Burger King, Orville Redenbacher, Oreo, SunChips, and more (Figure 10.1).

The idea itself was fun and the tweets were executed well, but the added bonus was that many of the brands responded with their own snarky responses, reaching beyond the Honda followers and also earning stories in places such as *Forbes*, *Fast Company*, *AdAge*, and *Branding Magazine*.

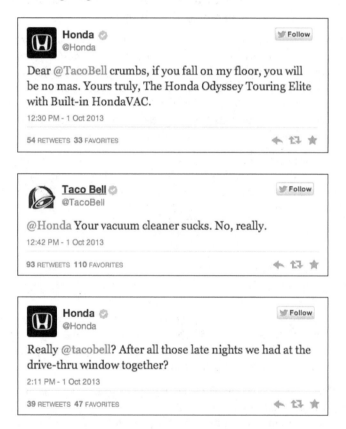

Figure 10.1   *Honda tweeted to promote their new in-car vacuum, and Taco Bell responded.*

When Oreo tweeted during the Super Bowl, we immediately saw the brand as more than a cookie. It now has a personality, like Big Bird or Oscar the Grouch. We like Oreo more now because of it. And, because so few brands are doing anything different or interesting online, it became news. The media relations team didn't have to call media to say, "Hey, are you interested in what we tweeted during the Super Bowl?" The publicity grew organically, very quickly, and Oreo had a viral hit on its hands.

Honda very carefully and strategically launched its ads and then the social element, and from that combination grew the earned media. They earned it not from multiyear relationships and staying top-of-mind with strategically placed phone calls, but through interesting online conversations that caught the attention of bloggers and journalists around the globe.

The future of communications is to work with a team that has a deep understanding of your brand so they can represent you live. Your culture must be about experimentation, and you must be willing to take some risk. These case studies don't come from being conservative and safe. They come from being able to tolerate failure, quickly pivot, and try again.

PR Becomes More Tangible

In October 2012, Bliss Integrated Marketing Communications announced they are no longer a PR firm. We did the very same thing in January of 2010. In April 2013, FleishmanHillard announced they are bringing all media under one roof and, in October 2013, Burson-Marsteller did the same.

The trend among communications firms is to focus on more than just earned media—so clients can hire one organization, get them ingrained into the business as deeply as if they are employed there, and give them the keys to the customer-facing doors. It used to be PR professionals were hired for their relationships with the media. Today they are hired for their skills in communicating with customers, prospects, critics, *and* shareholders.

The habits of consumers have changed. While many still receive the newspaper at home, it's rare they actually read it. We get our news—particularly breaking news—via text, Twitter, Facebook, or through other online outlets. Think about that from your own perspective. Where were you when you learned about the Boston bombings? How did you get your updates? Have you noticed, when there is a big storm in your area, that you suddenly began receiving severe weather alerts on your phone? Do you have a Twitter feed set up just for the news you want to receive? We each get our information in different ways, and it no longer fits to think solely about TV, radio, and print.

In the late 1990s, PRSA created two formulas to measure the effectiveness of media relations. They were implemented industry-wide and are still used today by many professionals. These formulas calculated media impressions and advertising equivalencies. For the media impressions, take the circulation of a publication and multiply it by five if it is a trade magazine, and by two and a half if it is a consumer publication. For instance, if your trade industry magazine has 30,000 subscribers, the media impressions are 150,000, the idea being that the magazine is easily routed around an office where an average of five people see it. The flaw in that, of course, is you may subscribe and never read it, or you may never read the article about the company in it. So 150,000 *potential* impressions is really the metric.

But, because the industry had never had a numerical way to measure its effectiveness, it took off. The finance executives appreciated having numbers they could attach to an expense line item. The chief executives appreciated having numbers—and big ones—they could show their boards.

Coupled with media impressions was the advertising equivalency. If you ran an ad in the same spot and the same size as the story that ran, how much would it have cost you? For instance, if you ran a quarter page ad below the fold on the front page of the *Wall Street Journal*, it would cost far more than what you paid your PR team to get the story in the same spot. The flaw there, of course, is that you can't buy space in that spot *and* it doesn't account for credibility.

Today executives still ask for those numbers because they're what they've become accustomed to seeing these past 20 years, and they're the numbers to show in presentations. In the information age, however, there are so many real ways to measure your effectiveness that media impressions and advertising equivalencies no longer make sense.

Analytics continue to improve every year and that won't change. Right now we can make fairly sound estimates of how much revenue is associated with marketing, communications, advertising, sales, customer service, or other channels that affect your organization's growth. But the analytics, at the surface level, are still vanity metrics: How many people visit your site, how many are new visitors, and how long they stay on a certain page. Communicators will have to get better at digging below the surface level to get smarter with their data and use the insights from it.

There is a great commercial from Adobe Marketing Cloud on YouTube. It shows a marketing person at Encyclopedia Atlantica receiving information that someone is buying hundreds of thousands of encyclopedias. He runs into the chief executive's office and shows him the report. The CEO gets on the phone with their manufacturing plant in China exclaiming, "We're back! We're back!" The manufacturing plant begins to print and ship encyclopedias. Then it cuts to a baby on the floor, with a tablet in front of him. He keeps pushing the "buy" button on the company's online ad while his parents lovingly say, "He sure does love that thing."

The metrics are available, but we can't take them at the surface level. Just as it doesn't make sense 150,000 people saw the story about your product in a trade magazine, it's pretty likely encyclopedias won't come back from the dead in a few short hours.

Content Marketing Evolves

In the information age, we all have so much coming at us at every second of the day. We often make judgments on companies, products, services, charities we'll support, and events we want to attend solely by the headline of the content they're producing to gain our attention. That whole "don't judge a book by its cover" is precisely what we do hundreds of times every day.

Because there is so much out there, a backlash about content marketing is building up. In the future, it will only get louder because companies continue to create really bad content. And when they realize they're terrible at executing the tactic, they decide content doesn't work—instead of realizing they're terrible at executing the tactic. Despite the backlash, competent communicators who create interesting, valuable, and engaging content will thrive and will be in high demand. Executives will look to fill their teams with those who have a proven history of not only flawless content creation, but its delivery and monetization as well.

Google will continue to place more emphasis on not just new content, but on how much it's shared, and how many people engage with it either on your site or on the social networks. Because of that, getting it right is imperative.

Of course, content marketing isn't new. John Deere launched their customer magazine, *The Furrow*, in 1895. In the early 1900s P&G, Sears, Michelin, and JELL-O joined the content fray. In the late 80s, LEGO created a customer publication focused on showcasing how their product is used in people's homes—other than sleepy, barefoot parents stepping on loose blocks in the middle of the night. In 2007, 7 out of 10 publications on U.K. newsstands were produced by corporations.

It's a trend that is as old as the cavemen and it's not going away anytime soon. But organizations that are bad at content creation will be very vocal in saying it doesn't work, and certain executives will take notice.

A 2013 study by Content Marketing Institute and MarketingProfs showed 93 percent of marketers are using content marketing, but more than half either don't have a documented content strategy or don't know if they do. You can't run your organization without a strategy and a clear vision, and the same is true for content marketing…or any marketing or communications, for that matter. If this study is indicative of the larger business world, it's clear why it's not working for so many.

There are four techniques that, if executed flawlessly, will help any organization—no matter what size, industry, or profit versus nonprofit—generate qualified leads and convert them into customers, donors, or stakeholders.

1. **Clear vision content.** In Chicago, there is a cab driver who calls himself Chicago Cabbie. In fact, his Twitter handle is @chicagocabbie. Rashid Temuri started using Twitter to provide Chicagoans an easy way to reserve a cab. You can tweet or direct-message him for an immediate pickup or to schedule a ride. His tweets show his current location so you know if he's two blocks or two miles away. Sure, you can call the cab companies and have the same kind of service, but what set him apart immediately is that he accepted credit cards. If you've ever tried to pay for a cab ride in Chicago with anything but cash, you know how hit-or-miss it is. Sometimes cab drivers will take your credit card; more often, though, they will get very upset with you for not having cash.

He was very forward-thinking. He used Square with his tablet so he could accept credit cards and bypass the high fees. As he gained popularity—he's something of a legend in Chicago—he began to add other services. When you reserve a ride, he sends you an invite so it's on your calendar. You can follow him on Foursquare so you know if he's close enough to pick you up. And, when he's not driving, he provides traffic, movie, restaurants, weather, lane closures, and events updates.

All his content is in bite-sized chunks because it's on Twitter, but he's become *the* source for anything there is to know about Chicago. If you're a native, it's almost easier to check his Twitter stream for traffic and lane closure news than the actual news sites. If you're visiting, you can tweet him and ask for restaurant recommendations in a particular neighborhood and he'll respond immediately.

He has a clear vision: Be a trusted resource about all things Chicago. In return, his business grew 20 percent the first year, he took a job with Hailo when it launched in Chicago, and he trains cab drivers, new and experienced alike, on how to use social media to grow their clientele.

2. **Brand journalism.** In 2007, American Express launched OPEN Forum as a way to support small businesses across the United States. When they launched, they invited experts—such as Guy Kawasaki and Pete Cashmore of Mashable—to provide commentary on small business growth, opportunities, and challenges.

   Business owners know how challenging it is to not only set up an organizational structure from a legal perspective, but to grow it by becoming an expert in finances, human resources, marketing, sales, product development, leadership, and more. The site was launched with the sole purpose of helping entrepreneurs who don't have the expertise—or easy access to the experts—learn how to do the things they need to do to stay in business.

   Brand journalism puts the storytelling in the hands of corporations. While you still want third-party influencers to tell your story for you, you no longer have to depend on it. American Express took this notion and built their story with the help of small business experts. Even if you're not an American Express cardholder, you can visit OPEN Forum and gain invaluable information on how to run your business. The benefit to the credit card company? Increased brand awareness and credibility, which brings people back to something they own, giving Amex the opportunity to track where visitors spend their time, and also work on converting those visitors to card holders.

3. **Sponsored stories.** On BuzzFeed—a website that provides a snapshot of the viral Web in real time—sponsored stories are part of the reader's experience. Visit their home page, and you will see things such as "22 NBA Players You Secretly Think You're Better Than," "11 Places You Need To Go Before You Die," and "If Carrie From 'Sex And The City' Had Instagram."

   Which story is sponsored?

It's hard to tell from reading the headlines because BuzzFeed does a phenomenal job of making sure their sponsors and advertisers don't sound sales-y, and don't violate the integrity of the site's design. The story has the same-sized image as the others on the site, its headline is snappy like the others, and the content reads exactly like one of the nonsponsored posts. The only difference? The "sponsored by" sentence underneath the headline.

Remember the advertorials of old? You would open a magazine and read an interesting story, only to learn it was paid for by a corporation. Sponsored stories are the advertorials of today, and they're effective because they look and feel just like the rest of the content on the site.

(For the record, the sponsored post is "11 Places You Need To Go Before You Die," which T-Mobile paid for.)

4. **Employee or customer stories.** An organization in Omaha, Neb., hires only visually impaired people. The business makes a product so intricate, it's impossible for people with sight to build it because we're too easily distracted. A conversation with their CEO revealed one of his employees climbed Mt. Hood unassisted, and another is one of the top gospel music vocalists in the world. It's interesting enough that they employ blind people; it's even more interesting when you learn such fascinating stories about their employees.

   REI, the outdoor recreation gear retail chain, is an organization that tells their employee stories extremely well. Go into any store and you'll see photos of their employees rock-climbing, running, biking, swimming, camping, and skiing on the walls near the cash registers. They hire people who have a passion for the outdoors, and therefore use their products with or without the job. That passion comes through in their personal lives, so the stories REI tells from the employee perspective make them look compelling and interesting.

   But it's not just employees who can make your business interesting. Customers can help draw you into a company's corporate story also. This is akin to the testimonial of old—but instead of placing a quote and the customer's name on your website, the storytelling is directly about the people who buy from you.

   Salesforce is an organization that does this well. If you visit their website, you'll find pages and pages of customer stories. What's interesting though is the testimonials are less about Salesforce—certainly not in a pushy way—and more about the customers' companies, and how they're growing by using the Salesforce software. The stories are linked directly to the customer's websites, social networks, and the Salesforce products they use.

   For instance, Chipotle talks about how they've used social media to connect directly with their customers, and you can like their Facebook page directly from there. Delta tells the story of how important it is for their customer service representatives to have all of the information when someone calls in about a flight. And Pandora has found new ways to enhance the listener experience and create new ad products and placements. Overall, we learn about the companies themselves, but we also come away knowing how much using the Salesforce software has helped them succeed.

Customer experience, real-time marketing, more tangible results, and evolving content represent the future of communications. And that future is now.

Index

Gini **Dietrich**

SPIN Sucks

FREE
Online Edition

Safari
Books Online

Your purchase of *Spin Sucks* includes access to a free online edition for 45 days through the **Safari Books Online** subscription service. Nearly every Que book is available online through **Safari Books Online**, along with thousands of books and videos from publishers uch as Addison-Wesley Professional, Cisco Press, Exam Cram, IBM Press, O'Reilly Media, Prentice Hall, and Sams.

Safari Books Online is a digital library providing searchable, on-demand access to thousands of technology, digital media, and professional development books and videos from leading publishers. With one monthly or yearly subscription price, you get unlimited access to learning tools and information on topics including mobile app and software development, tips and tricks on using your favorite gadgets, networking, project management, graphic design, and much more.

Activate your FREE Online Edition at informit.com/safarifree

STEP 1:   Enter the coupon code: AVQGXBI.

STEP 2:   New Safari users, complete the brief registration form. Safari subscribers, just log in.

If you have diff culty registering on Safari or accessing the online edition, please e-mail customer-service@safaribooksonline.com